# RURAL RAM

## *near Bristo*

## *Bath*

*Other walking titles around the Bristol and Bath area available from Countryside Books include:*

Teashop Walks Around Bristol and Bath

Pub Strolls Around Bristol and Bath

Pub Walks near Bristol and Bath

Kiddiwalks Around Bristol and Bath

On Your Bike Around Bristol and Bath

Waterside Walks near Bristol and Bath

Pub Walks Along the Kennet and Avon Canal

# RURAL RAMBLES
## *near Bristol and Bath*

Connie Smith and Richard Harris

COUNTRYSIDE BOOKS

NEWBURY, BERKSHIRE

First published as *Walks in Avon*, 1981
by Spurbooks

Completely revised and updated 1992
**This new edition published 2004**

COUNTRYSIDE BOOKS
3 Catherine Road
Newbury, Berkshire

ISBN 1 85306 851 9

To view our complete range of books
please visit us at
www.countrysidebooks.co.uk

Cover photograph of Blagdon Lake, supplied by Bill Meadows
Photographs by Richard Harris

Produced through MRM Associates Ltd., Reading
Typeset by Mac Style Ltd, Scarborough, N. Yorkshire
Printed by J.W. Arrowsmith Ltd., Bristol

# Contents

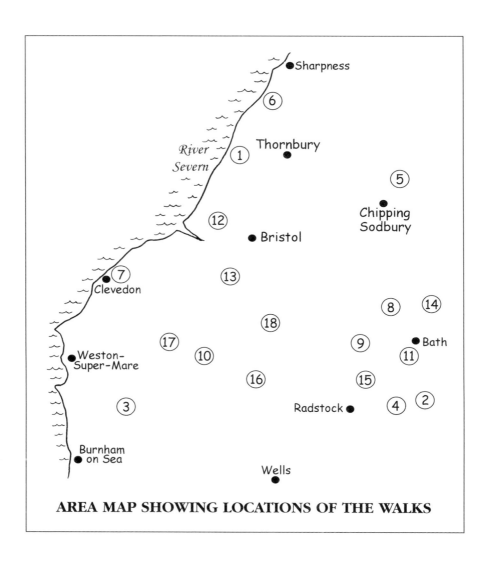

**AREA MAP SHOWING LOCATIONS OF THE WALKS**

## PUBLISHER'S NOTE

We hope that you obtain considerable enjoyment from this book; great care has been taken in its preparation. Although at the time of publication all routes followed public rights of way or permitted paths, diversion orders can be made and permissions withdrawn.

We cannot, of course, be held responsible for such diversion orders and any inaccuracies in the text which might result from these or any other changes to the routes nor any damage which might result from walkers trespassing on private property. We are anxious though that all details covering the walks are kept up to date and would therefore welcome information from readers which would be relevant to future editions.

The simple sketch maps that accompany the walks in this book are based on notes made by the authors whilst checking out the routes on the ground. They are designed to show you how to reach the start, to point out the main features of the overall circuit and they contain a progression of numbers that relate to the paragraphs of the text.

However, for the benefit of a proper map, we do recommend that you purchase the relevant Ordnance Survey sheet covering your walk. The Ordnance Survey maps are widely available, especially through booksellers and local newsagents.

# INTRODUCTION

The former county of Avon was created by the 1974 Local Government reorganisation, taking its name from the river which crosses the county. From the east, the Avon enters two miles from Bradford-on-Avon. It flows through the Georgian city of Bath and then the heart of Bristol before making its exit into the Severn estuary on the western side. To the north-east and south of the county, the limestone uplands of the Cotswolds and the Mendips rise over 600 ft. On the other extreme, there are coastal plains and levels to the west where large tracts lie only a little above sea level. In between the north and the south are hills, low plateaux and undulating country, while around Bath oolite limestone hills are divided by narrow valleys. In the centre, running in a north/south direction, lies a rolling landscape associated with the now extinct Bristol and North Somerset coalfields.

These walks are designed to highlight some of the many attractive areas that await the country user who looks for the simple pleasures to be found in the open air. The agricultural scene contains a wealth of quiet villages and hamlets, all waiting to be discovered. Walking is a leisure pursuit for all ages which is gaining in popularity all the time – increased mobility encourages this healthy pastime.

Each walk lists the OS maps that are recommended for use in conjunction with the detailed instructions. The sketch maps are included for guidance only and are not drawn to scale, but a compass bearing taken from these maps is generally accurate enough. Some people may find that the walks will provide ideas for outings that may have not been previously thought of – for others perhaps it will boost confidence in having a go. This country's footpaths and bridleways represent a priceless heritage that has been handed down from countless people who have used them for many purposes. We are privileged to walk them and, if we continue to do so, then they will be preserved for those who may follow.

Connie Smith and Jean Finlayson wrote the above words for the first edition of this book, which they compiled together in 1992.

For my part, I began using this book after pneumonia left me decidedly short of breath. Then I arranged with Countryside Books to revise the walks. Some six months and eighteen walks later, I consider I have literally walked my way back to health. In my opinion, rambling is one of the most exciting and fun ways to take exercise because you can start at any level and participate at your own pace. If you are completely new to walking, all you need to get going on the walks is the clothes you stand up in and this book.

I had terrific fun revising the walks, with the help of my friend Michael Seales, and we, together with Connie, hope you will gain as much pleasure from them as we have.

Richard Harris

# OLDBURY ON SEVERN AND THE BRISTOL CHANNEL

*Thornbury Yacht Club*

The shoreline of the Vale of Berkeley overlooks the sparkling Severn estuary and the enchanting distant skyline of the rising Welsh hills. This flat and easy-going walk is through green meadows, with narrow lanes and small, pretty hamlets. The wealth of mature trees shows that the pastures were won from the low-lying marshland a very long time ago. The hedgerows are full of tall reeds masking drainage channels (rhines), which help to keep the land in good fettle. From the sea wall, dividing the saltings from the fertile farmland, the mud flats can be seen. They are rich in marine life and attract many species of wading bird.

- **HOW TO GET THERE:** By car – Littleton on Severn lies 3 miles west of Thornbury. Take the A38 for 10 miles north of Bristol, then the B4061 to Thornbury. From High Street pass downhill into Castle Street, passing the town pump in a wrought iron cage. Thornbury church is ahead. Look for a turning left, Kington Lane, signposted to the cemetery and Munday playing fields. Follow the occasional sign to Littleton and park on the southern side (passing the White Hart on the left) outside the parish hall.
- **LENGTH OF THE WALK:** 6 miles, which will take 2 to 3 hours. Maps: OS Landranger 172 Bristol & Bath or OS Explorer 167 Thornbury, Dursley and Yate (GR 595899).

## THE WALK

**1.** With your back to the parish hall, walk along the village street past the post box and the Evangelical church opposite. Pass the telephone box and after another 20 yards climb the stone stile to a footpath on the left. No signpost now, just the grey pole. The stile is opposite an orange brick house. Follow the hedge on your right and then go through a gate between a barn and a farmhouse. There is a faint path to the gate ahead with a stile alongside. Maintain direction through the middle of the next field where there is a double stile and plank bridge over a ditch. Continue with a hedge on your left to the next stile in the corner of the field, then go diagonally right in the fifth field to a stile hidden in the hedgerow about 15 yards from the far corner. It is another double one with ditch and plank. Turn right and walk with the hedge on the right. Climb the gate at the far end into a lane.

**2.** Turn left for a few yards, and then turn right into a bridleway. It is lined with the occasional oak tree and ends in a gate. There is a good view here of the Oldbury power station. Continue forward – the track is now open on your left. Head towards a willow-shrouded pond and here turn left across the field towards a gate in the opposite hedge. At the gate continue through the next field as before to a stile, in the far left corner of the field. It gives access to an elaborate footbridge across a rhine. The sea wall is on the other side.

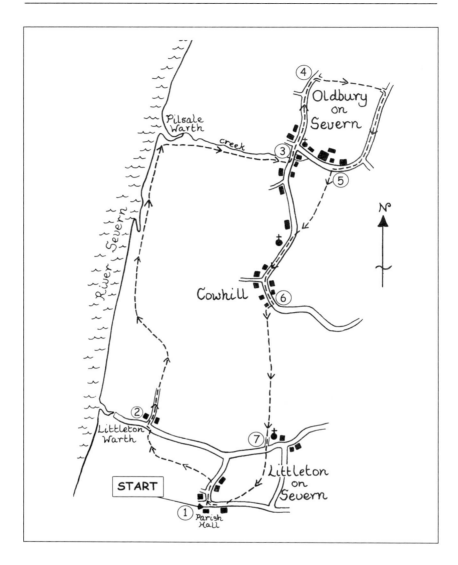

Here is the place to stop and take in the excellent views of the distant motorway bridges over the Severn. Chepstow can be seen and also the Sedbury cliffs from where the Offa's Dyke long distance footpath begins. Oldbury power station dominates the northern scene with Oldbury church upon its eminence alongside.

Turn right along the sea wall embankment. First comes Pillhead Gout and then Pilsale Gout where the path along the embankment bends inland opposite to the yacht clubhouse and its moorings. As the embankment swings left to meet the sluice gates turn half right and drop down from the embankment. Continue forward with the creek on your left and a wire fence to your right. It will take you to the southern end of Oldbury village by way of the stiled horse paddock and pony stables.

**3.** Turn left into Church Road. Walk through pleasant Oldbury village past the Anchor. At the road junction go straight on along Camp Road (also signposted to West End cul-de-sac). Pass by the Ship inn and the narrow War Memorial Hall. Notice the houses on the right-hand side of the road are elevated upon a bank, the last vestige of the ancient Iron Age camp from which Oldbury takes its name.

*The Anchor at Oldbury*

**4.** At the Ham Lane junction by 'The Villa' turn right into West End. Pass by the cottages, after which the lane becomes an enclosed track with an uneven grass surface. Follow it to its end. It becomes metalled just before the road junction. Turn right into The Naite. Thornbury church tower on the left can be seen above the green trees. After about $1/4$ mile turn right into Chapel Road. Another $1/4$ mile will take you to the entrance of Priest Orchard House (opposite Rook Farm).

**5.** Turn left over the concrete rhine bridge. Almost opposite the end of the bridge, go through a swing gate. Ignore the new waymarked path alongside the rhine which goes to the Anchor. St Arilda's church now stands ahead and dominates the scene on Cow Hill. Walk towards it. There is a hedge on the right; shortly pass through a new kissing gate next to a stile. Carry on up to the top right corner and a second new swing gate. Diagonally ahead again is a third swing gate and the road. On the left of the church is the rectory and on the right is a 19th century school. Follow the road up to the church and enter the churchyard. There are seats invitingly placed for you to pause and enjoy the lovely views. Around the other side of the church are stone steps and a swing gate to take you back into the road.

After $1/4$ mile a small cluster of buildings called Cowhill is reached. Pass the red letterbox.

**6.** Almost immediately on the right and after a cottage, which stands sidewise on to the road, go through the garden gate which is waymarked and has painted on it 'Littleton 1 mile'. (It is directly opposite the entrance to Church View Farm.) The waymark points the way through a small overgrown orchard. Slightly left is a stile and a field beyond. Follow the left-hand hedgerow, passing under the electricity wires, up a very large field, possibly heavily planted with tall sweet corn to the far end. Continue up the hill still with the hedge on the left. Where the hedge drops away, make for the corner of the wood in front of you, passing it on your left-hand side to the brow of the hill. Here turn left through a gate into a field. Littleton will come into view. Follow the path; the wood is still on your left.

Continue along the wood's edge and pass over a stile into the church access lane (the church is on the left).

**7.** When the road is reached cross straight over and go through the waymarked gate. Soon another gate into a large field is reached. Follow the waymark and go slightly right past the red-tile roofed house into the field corner. Cross the double stile (waymarked). Above you are some electricity wires; pass under them and walk with them on your right for a short distance, then follow the hedge on your right to the corner of the field. At the triangle of rough grass turn slightly left to pass under the ash tree. It lies on the field boundary but there is no stile or wire, so follow the right-hand hedge to the stile in the far corner of the next field and the road. Turn right in the road and pass by Northly Farm on your right to bring you back to your car.

*Refreshments:* There are plenty of cafes and pubs in Thornbury, as well as pubs in Littleton (the White Hart) and Oldbury (the Anchor and the Ship).

NOTES

**Littleton Warth:** The extremely high and ferocious tides of the Bristol Channel, combined with low-lying marshland, caused Littleton and Oldbury to be built not on the shoreline but a mile or so inland at the head of a tidal creek. These waterways are called warths, gouts or pills. In 1885 Littleton Warth gained a new name when a whale was stranded there. For a time it hit the headlines and a new name of Whale Wharf appeared. Today Littleton Warth has regained its former title and its small boating business has been absorbed into a trading estate.

**Oldbury on Severn** is scattered. The core straddles an Iron Age fort at one time called 'the Toots'. The parish church stands upon its own detached knoll. It has a dedication to a local Saxon saint, Arilda, which provides proof of its antiquity, though the present building goes back only about 100 years. The Oldbury nuclear power station has a visitor centre for pre-booked visits.

**The Severn Bridge** is the seventh longest in the world. It was opened in 1966 to a design of Sir Gilbert Roberts. It has been compared to Brunel's suspension bridge in Bristol some 10 miles distant, for each in its day represented a pinnacle of achievement in steel and wrought iron. Behind is the Second Severn Crossing, with a total length of 5.1km and opened in 1996. This bridge is located near the Severn Tunnel. There is a seasonal visitor centre open from Easter.

Upstream the Severn Bore or Egre occurs when the incoming water flows over the top of the river and produces a wave sometimes as much as 6 ft high.

# THE MIDFORD VALLEY
# AND HINTON CHARTERHOUSE

*The goblet shaped water tower*

The picturesque valleys of the Wellow and Cam typify the green and hilly countryside south of Bath and though both were used to take away the coal produced in the Somerset coalfield, passing time has healed any scars and what remains is an interesting reminder of our working past. From Hinton Charterhouse, the walk passes near to the Carthusian priory, where the scant ruins have been carefully preserved. There is a drop down into the Midford valley, with its disused railways and coal canal. Much of the lining of the narrow cut has crumbled and brambles fill the gaps. After climbing over the hill, you reach the Wellow valley. Both valleys are very quiet and the only noises are agricultural and bird song, including the nightingale.

- **HOW TO GET THERE:** By bus: the Bath/Frome service passes through Hinton Charterhouse and calls hourly on weekdays. From the bus stop, walk eastwards along the village street in the direction of the church. By car: Hinton Charterhouse is on the B3110 Bath/Norton St Philip road, 1 mile west of the A36 Bath/Warminster road (some 8 miles south of Bath). Parking may be found on the north side of the village in the cricket ground, which is behind the Rose & Crown pub. On the B3110 from Bath, turn left into Branch Road (signposted Warminster A36, Frome A361) and shortly right at the footpath sign. With the back of the cricket pavilion to your left and the children's playground (near to the practice nets) on your right, walk towards the housing. There is a footpath through a broken swing gate and an enclosed way under an archway into Green Lane. Turn left for the start of the walk.
- **LENGTH OF THE WALK:** 6 miles, taking 3 to $3^{1}/_{2}$ hours. Maps: OS Landranger 172 Bristol & Bath, or OS Explorer 142 Shepton Mallet & Mendip East and Explorer 155 Bristol & Bath, Keynsham/Marshfield (GR 770583).

### THE WALK

**1.** To reach the church of St John the Baptist, continue with the stone wall on your left. Follow it past the Jubilee seat and Hinton House entrance until it eventually turns left. It leads past the cattle pound to the churchyard gate. Inside the churchyard, the beautiful 13th century church will be on your left-hand side. Follow the gravel path, which bends to the right, and then take the grassy path with goes towards the far corner of the churchyard to meet a wall. Follow the walling (on your left) and go through the swing gate at the end of the churchyard, followed immediately by a stile. In the very large meadow beyond, walk forwards over the slight rise towards the clump of tall conifers which are at first half hidden by the rise in the ground. To the left is stately early 18th century Hinton House.

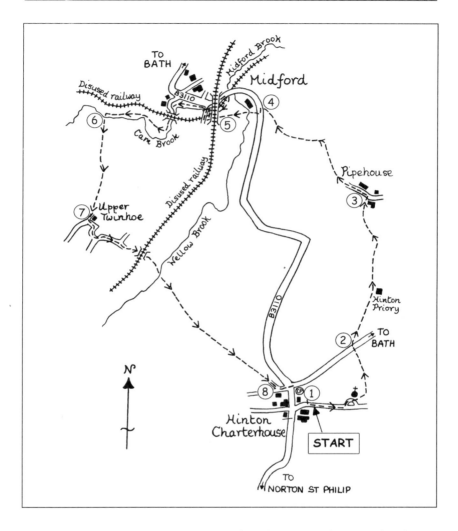

Pass by the conifers on your left-hand side and cross the fence by a stile. Continue forwards to the long line of trees. At a gap in the tree line, you will see a field gate and stile.

**2.** Cross the stile and go straight over the road. Enter the new swing gate opposite. The fingerpost points the way half right across the next field. The ruins of Charterhouse Priory will be seen in the far meadow. As you approach the distant side of the field, head for the stile which is to the right of the tall ash tree and about 30 yards from the corner of the field. After the stile continue in the direction marked and pass close to a spinney on your left. As the spinney drops away, maintain your direction to the stile in the fence straight ahead. The ruins are now close by on your right (in the next meadow). Follow the right-hand hedge a short distance to the stile and climb over. The next stile is plainly in view a little to the right of a small copse. After the stile, a footpath passes along the centre of a cultivated field. Cross into the next field gradually closing up to the left-hand hedge as you walk towards the poultry farm building ahead of you. The general direction is towards a double electricity pole with a transformer. Climb over a stile and walk the next field (hedge on left). Two more stiles will take you over a farm track. The poultry farm is now on the right. Pass through a small paddock with a stile at each end (to the right of the double electricity pole) and a short enclosed way next to a house garden to reach the lane and Pipehouse hamlet.

**3.** Turn left. Note the chapel and 'Village Room' dated 1903 on the right, now converted into a handsome house. At the end of the small hamlet, pass by a very fine thatched house. Thatch is not so common hereabouts. The lane becomes a track. After a few hundred yards, where a right fork leads to the goblet-shaped water tower, go straight forward. The track now deteriorates into a narrow, steep and rough wet way as it goes down to Midford in the valley below. It is a mile to the B3110 (Bath/Norton St Philip road). The way is enclosed but now and again there are tantalising glimpses of the pleasant countryside.

**4.** At the road, cross over and turn left along the pavement. After a few yards, turn right at the end of the mill buildings. A steel footbridge will take you over the Wellow brook into the meadow at the base of the valley. The walk now goes west along the valley for a while. A long raised ridge in the field guides you towards the disused railway viaduct just visible in the trees on the far side of the large meadow, closing up with the Cam brook,

*The Hope & Anchor inn, Midford*

which is on your right. It is a good place to listen for the nightingale. Climb the stile onto a short track.

**5.** Pass under the tall viaduct onto the road. Turn right. Pass by a second dismantled railway bridge to the T-junction with the B3110 in Midford once more. Turn right. After a few yards, turn right onto a footpath opposite the Hope & Anchor inn. The waymarked footpath goes under the railway viaduct and a road. The bed of the old coal canal is on the left. This section has been made into a very lovely, long and narrow garden. At the end, a swing gate will take you across the bed of the canal through a scrubby area. As the field opens out, you will see that you are walking along the raised towpath of the disused canal (now on the right). On the left is the ruinous bridge over the Cam brook which once formed the beginning of the Radstock arm of the coal canal. Soon you will see a much smaller, hump-back bridge on your right.

Soon, the well-walked path reaches the disused railway embankment. Pass through a swing gate and follow the path as it goes left to pass under the embankment bridge near to the Cam. Follow the path through another swing gate, which gives access to the valley meadow and the raised canal towpath, with the canal on your right once more. This is a beautiful valley that takes you west for another $^1/_2$ to $^3/_4$ mile. The path ends with steps and a metal gate onto a cross track.

**6.** Turn left and cross the Cam by the footbridge. The direction is now southwards up over the hill and into the Wellow valley. The track, narrow at first, broadens to a stony track, leading to the top and through a wooden farm gate to Upper Twinhoe Farm. Here you will want to pause and take in the views in all directions. The track ends in a T-junction.

**7.** Turn left into the lane. At the junction, turn left again. After 300 yards, pass Leesons Cottage and turn right at the guidepost to the entrance to Middle Twinhoe Barns. Bear left immediately before the entrance to the house. A very short track goes to a gate and stile alongside the first barn.

Climb the stile and follow the left-hand hedge to a gate. The direction marker points towards the corner of the next field, half left, but if this field is very overgrown, follow the boundary walls to the gate in the bottom left corner. From here may be seen the red tiled roofs of stone buildings. On your right is the Wellow valley, with Hinton Charterhouse visible on the distant skyline.

From this waymarked gatepost, follow close to the hedge on your right into the field for just a couple of yards; the way is now an overgrown, rough, grassy track, narrow at first between banks dropping below field level, that leads down into the Wellow valley. After a gate, pass by the garden of Lower Twinhoe Farm. At the T-junction, turn right and continue downwards.

On reaching the railway arch, ignore the fork on the right and go down under the archway where there is a gate. On the other side, a clear fenced path half right leads downhill to the Wellow brook. Go through another gate; the track swings right and follows the stream on the left. Continue in the same direction and follow the bank along to the gated footbridge.

Turn left over the bridge. Resume your direction and immediately drop down, over the plank bridge on your left, into Twinhoeford Wood. Turn right along the edge of the wood for about 150 yards, with the stream on your right-hand side. Look for a second plank bridge and re-cross the stream. Resume your direction and go through a gate out of the wood and into a meadow.

Your way is now up out of the Wellow valley towards Hinton Charterhouse. Go through the combe, narrow at first, with a stream and scrub on your left. Presently it broadens out and after three large meadows and two gates the way ends at a hunting gate to the right of two houses.

**8.** A short track then goes between the houses into a narrow metalled lane between high banks and then steeply up into Hinton Charterhouse. Turn left past The Homestead to reach the B3110. Cross straight over to return to the car park and, after a short distance, turn right into the cricket field. Bus users should turn right onto the B3110 and walk past the Stag public house to the bus stop.

*Refreshments:* The Stag and the Rose & Crown, both in Hinton Charterhouse, serve food every day, both lunchtime and evening (no food on Sunday evening at the Stag). There is also the Hope and Anchor in Midford. All three pubs offer excellent menus.

## NOTES

**Hinton Charterhouse** is a village of two parts, which stands at one of the highest points in the Avon area, south of Bristol. It had its beginnings not on the B3110 road but a little to the east where a church was built as soon as the community could support one. St James' church has fragments of Norman Romanesque stonework in the north doorway to prove that there was a thriving community in the 11th century.

By the 13th century the name had changed from Hantone to Hinton. Ella, Countess of Salisbury, then fulfilled her dead husband's wishes and founded the Carthusian priory. The very strict religious settlement was sited about 1 mile north-east of

Hinton village and, since such monks call their monasteries 'Charterhouse', then Hinton became Hinton Charterhouse. The collection of houses, with two inns at the crossroads, came with the increase in road travel in the 17th and 18th centuries.

**Midford** stands at the confluence of the Cam and Wellow brooks. At the beginning of the 19th century, these brooks were used to fill the Somerset Coal Canal, which was designed in two cuts from basins at Paulton and Radstock. Barges took the coal to the Kennet and Avon Canal near to the Dundas aqueduct in the Avon valley for transportation elsewhere. The Radstock arm of the waterway proved to be unsuccessful and a tramway along the cut was substituted in 1815. Eventually, when the Somerset Coal Canal ceased business and was liquidated, the GWR stepped in and built the Camerton/Limpley Stoke single line railway (1907–1951). Part of the canal bed was used and the rest left to moulder away and grow green as nature took over. One small section has been excavated near to the Dundas aqueduct egress which today serves as a leisure craft marina.

Midford has altered many times. The last change came with the building of the Somerset & Dorset Railway between Bath and the south of England in 1874. The track pierced Midford from the north, passed over the canal and Camerton railway line, and continued to Radstock via Wellow, utilizing the tramroad. Midford station was perched against the rocky hillside with a single platform on the 'up' side. The remains may be seen from the car park of the Hope and Anchor public house.

# CROOK PEAK
# AND WAVERING DOWN

*View towards Cheddar Reservoir*

The West Mendip Way long distance footpath stretches between Uphill, near to Weston-super-Mare, and Wells. One splendid section where the Mendips fall away is in the extreme south-western corner of the old county of Avon and it provides an exhilarating ridge walk. From Winscombe, the path is steep but not too strenuous. On a clear day the panorama of coastal flats, inland country, and distant hills is well worth the effort of the climb.

- **HOW TO GET THERE:** By bus: There is an hourly service Monday to Saturday (two-hourly on Sunday) on the

Bristol/Weston-super-Mare route. Also an hourly service on weekdays between Weston, Winscombe, Cheddar and Wells. By car: Winscombe lies on the A371 Banwell/Winscombe road and near to the A38 Bristol/Burnham-on-Sea road. Parking may be found at the rear and side of the Woodborough Hotel.

- **LENGTH OF THE WALK:** 5 miles, about $3^1/_2$ hours. Maps: OS Landranger 182, or OS Explorer 141 Cheddar Gorge & Mendip Hills West and Explorer 153 Weston-super-Mare & Bleadon Hill (GR 420575).

### THE WALK

**1.** With your back to the Woodborough Hotel, walk forward in the direction of Banwell (A371 Winscombe/Banwell road) to the first junction (signposted to Barton and Loxton). On the left-hand side, near to the small triangular green, go over the stone stile between the houses. An enclosed path leads to an open field. Go forward to the next block of housing. Pass under the electric overhead cabling to the lane. Here, turn left and immediately right to resume your direction. The way is metalled at first and then beyond the houses it becomes a good footpath, with a wooden fence on the right. Follow the right-hand hedge after passing over a stone stile. A second stone stile under a horse chestnut tree about halfway along the hedge takes you into the next field.

There is a good view of Shute Shelve Hill to the left and to the right is the old village of Winscombe, with its church and fine stone tower rising above the surrounding trees under Wavering Down.

Continue forward through an iron gate. The hedge is now on your right and makes a sudden excursion left into the field. Walk round this to the stream and a wood plank-crossing place in the hedge. Walk half-left through the next field to a stile in open view. Cross the stile and turn right towards Winscombe church. There is also a tall wind pump that shows your direction. Walk diagonally across the field and through a gap in the top corner to pass to the top of the next and smaller field. The stile is in the hedge opposite, just to the left of some electricity wires that cross the hedge. The stile leads to the stream with stepping-stones in a dip. The enclosed path beyond you will pass close to the wind pump. Go over a stile into a green track. Continue in the same direction into Winscombe.

**2.** Turn left into Eastwell Lane. (Ignore the entrance to the new housing at Eastwell.) After about 100 yards, turn right into Church Lane to the parish church of St James. Go through an iron swing gate into the churchyard, where there is a good variety of trees both young and old, including the venerable tall yew with its circular seat. Pass the church on your left and walk out of the churchyard by way of a second iron swing gate.

The church lies in such a magnificent setting on the southern side of this delightful valley that you will be reluctant to leave. At the far side lie, from right to left, the hills of Lyncombe, Sandford and Banwell, then through the gap before Bleadon Hill peeps the housing of Weston-super-Mare.

Go forward with an orchard on your right. At the fork in the path, go left towards the woodland. A swing gate takes you into the wood. Go left again and climb upwards through the trees. This is called Church Knoll and forms part of the lower slopes of Wavering Down; In the springtime it is ablaze with bluebells and yellow celandines.

Very soon, after a small gully, take the narrow path uphill. Observe the waymark taking you left and up into the wood. It comes out on the edge of the wood where there is a steep bank with some trees and bracken on your immediate right. Climb the bank for a short distance until you can see the right corner of the sloping field. Continue diagonally up the field to the right-hand corner and a wooden stile. (There is a small wood shed on the left of the stile.) Turn right into Barton Drove.

From this elevated old track there is a good view of the Bristol Channel and beyond into distant Wales. Pass in front of a farmhouse. From this point the track becomes a field path with new wooden swing gates. A waymarked stile leads down into a field which you leave by another stile on your left. A fence is now on your right, passing some stables. The way becomes enclosed once more and shortly you pass a house in a

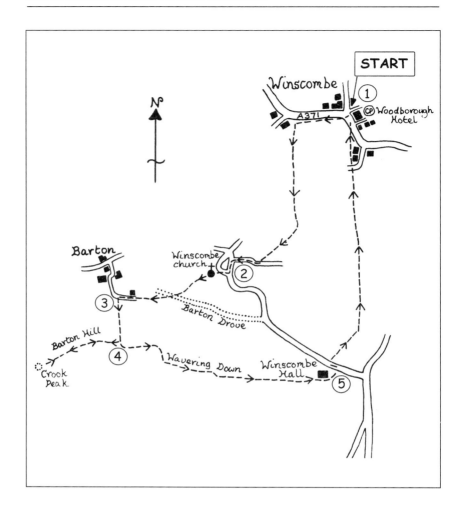

large garden on your right-hand side. Next comes a downward slope to a stile, after which you continue forward for about 75 yards.

**3.** At the boundary fence, turn sharp left. The walk now goes south to climb steeply up between Wavering Down and Compton Hill. There is a dent in the hillside on your left. Follow the waymarked fence steadily upwards. It ends at a stile at the top and brings you out onto the West Mendip Way.

**4.** Turn right and walk along the top of Compton Hill to Crook Peak ($^3/_4$ mile). After taking in your fill of the wonderful panorama stretching in all directions, retrace your steps to the point where you first reached the saddle between Compton Hill and Wavering Down. Continue forward and climb the last slope to the highest point on the down (211 m) at the triangulation station.

From here it is down, down, all the way. Follow the broad swathe of grass and head towards the trees. Walk past Hill Farm and, with the walling on your left, continue for another $^3/_4$ mile. Look left through the trees to the windowless gazebo built into the stone wall at the rear of Winscombe Hall Residential Home. Keeping the stone wall on your immediate left, continue downwards until you reach the National Trust car park. You are now at the foot of Wavering Down.

**5.** Turn left and walk back up the road for about 100 yards. Opposite the drive entrance to Winscombe Hall is a signpost; pass through a metal swing gate into the corner of a field. Head diagonally downwards to the corner of the wood opposite. Go round the corner to a waymarked stile on the left, and continue in the same direction to a stile in the next field corner. Cross a track and pass into the next field over a stile.

Winscombe church is again in the distance, this time to the left. Continue along the path through more fields, keeping the hedge on your right. At the far end of Winscombe Rugby Club field, turn into Yadley Lane and resume your direction. Pass by Yadley Close on the left. Shortly afterwards pick up the disused railway line on your right (now a walkway). Follow the well-worn path into Winscombe village. After about 600 yards and, just before the railway walkway passes over the main road, turn sharp left down some narrow steps in the hedge and walk along a short track into Woodborough Road. The location of these steps coincides with the far end of a cottage on the right that is very close to the side of the walkway. Once on the road, turn right to go under the bridge and you will see the Woodborough Hotel where you began the walk.

*Refreshments:* The Woodborough Hotel at the start of the walk.

NOTES

**Mendip limestone** has attracted stone-getters for a very long time. These people used to live around their stone workings which probably accounts for the straggling nature of older villages. Today, these old quarries are abandoned and Mendip stone is worked nearer to Cheddar and elsewhere in the district.

**Winscombe:** A railway from Cheddar in 1869 cleaved its way between the hills of Shute Shelve and Wavering Down on its way northwards. It bypassed the old hamlet of Winscombe and a station was built on the lower ground at Woodborough near to the main road junction. The railway station attracted its own housing settlement and, to confuse matters, it took on the name of Winscombe. Thus, today, the new Winscombe possesses a pub called the Woodborough, and old Winscombe, with its parish church, is isolated higher up on the hillside under Wavering Down to the south-west. Many villages in these parts have splendid churches with magnificent 15th century towers and Old Winscombe is no exception. St James the Great also possesses some beautifully carved wooden bench ends and 15th century stained glass.

**Wavering Down**, being a little higher than Crook Peak, is topped with a triangulation point, which is a concrete marker previously used by the Ordnance Survey as a sighting for map making purposes. Today, with bearings being made by aerial photography and satellite, these trig points are obsolete, though they can prove a comforting sight to country users who otherwise might be unsure of their whereabouts in unknown country.

# STONY LITTLETON LONG BARROW AND WELLOW

*The entrance to the long barrow*

A reminder of our Stone Age ancestors begins this delightful walk in the Wellow valley. Stony Littleton long barrow is the foremost tangible sign of Neolithic man which exists in this area. From the earthwork, the walk follows a figure of eight, with the charming village of Wellow at the centre point, a mile or so from the long barrow. This straggling village on the side of the valley has no appearance of being cocooned by the surrounding hills yet every approach is steep one way or the other.

- **HOW TO GET THERE:** By car: From the Bath/Radstock road (A367) follow the Wellow road. At Wellow High Street turn right and at the end of the village take the left turn signposted to the Long Barrow. It is then $^3/_4$ mile to the small parking place on the left of the lane opposite the stone cottage.

- **LENGTH OF THE WALK:** $5^1/_2$ miles, taking about 3 hours. Maps: OS Landranger 172 Bristol & Bath or OS Explorer 142 Shepton Mallet & Mendip Hills East (GR 734568).

### THE WALK

**1.** Walk over the Cam brook by the footbridge, turn left and cross over a stile. The brook falls away as you climb the hill (hedge on left). Halfway up is a stile and signpost to the long barrow. For a closer look follow the footpath and then return to this point (it is $^1/_2$ mile altogether). Currently you can actually view inside the barrow. At the top of the hill go through the gate and follow the well fertilized bridle path against the right-hand hedge.

From this elevated position the Cam valley may be seen to advantage. Behind, it meanders with the water through folds in

*View of Wellow from the long barrow*

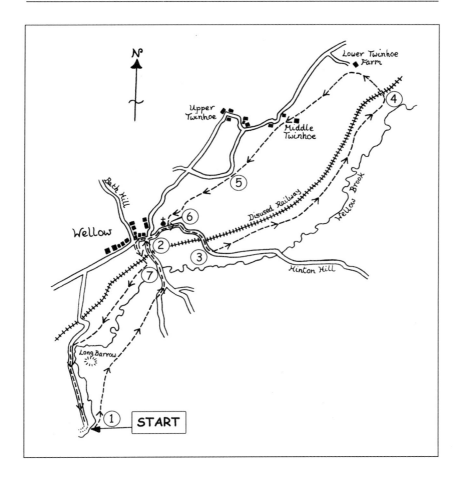

the hills. To the left is the long barrow on a spur of the hillside above the Cam brook. In front is Wellow with its church at the far end. Wellow lies up on the hillside above the valley bottom on the spring line where the impervious clay meets the limestone.

Where the hedge turns right continue forward through open cultivation to an enclosed track. Walk along the track for $1/2$ mile. At the end a lane comes in on the right. Go forward to the T-junction (Hassage Hill). Turn left down the hill towards Wellow. Pass by an old orchard (left) and then go over the quaint old bridge (or new ford) at the bottom. Walk up the hill into the village.

**2.** Turn right at the crossroads into the main street. Pass the village school (right) and then St Julian's church (left). Down the hill and round the bend in the dip go under the disused 3-arched railway viaduct. Pass by the Wellow Trekking Centre on the left and in 75 yards bear left on to a bank that follows the roadside at first. (It is immediately after a gate at a field entrance.)

**3.** Walk along the bank with a fence on the left. After a gate, continue alongside the fence. The well-used bridlepath contours the left side of the main valley. Where it meets a hedge boundary, walk to the left of it to the corner of the field to reach the trees. Go through a new gate in the corner and into Hankley Wood. The bridleway is now a rough, and often muddy, track for $^1/_4$ mile. At the far end of the old neglected coppiced wood the valley comes into view once again and the track goes downwards.

The valley is decidedly narrower here and winds towards the deciduous woods in front of you. Up on the skyline (forward and slightly left) lies Lower Twinhoe House, the next objective to be passed. In the meantime the track meets two gates in the bottom of the valley very near to the Cam brook.

**4.** At this point pass through the left gate and follow the fenced way up out of the valley and under the edge of the trees on the left. The trees mask the disused tall railway embankment. Turn left under the railway arch and through a gate to climb the steep hill. The stony track is enclosed and lined with many species of wild flowers that delight passers-by all through the flowering season.

At the T-junction under the garden of Lower Twinhoe House turn left up a green track passing soon through a gate. This is the halfway point of the walk, where you pass up and out of view of the Cam valley for a short while. It will now be seen that Lower Twinhoe House was on the slope of the hill and the green track leads up to Middle Twinhoe. The track emerges to field level; walk immediately ahead the few yards into the bottom corner of the next field. To reach Middle Twinhoe cross a cultivated field and paddock. The way is diagonally right to a waymarked gate, but if the field is very overgrown, follow the boundary fence and, after a left turn, with the boundary wall to your right, you will reach the gate at the end of the wall. Proceed towards the farm outbuildings across the paddock. Pass the nearest stable on your left-hand side. Go through a gate to pick up the entrance drive; turn right. After about 20 yards, pass by a field gate on the left and climb up to the elevated stile, which is a few yards further.

Walk through a field with the fence on your right-hand side. Pass through a gate and a second field with a young plantation in its far end. Climb the stile in the top corner. Resume your direction up and walk through the broad cultivations to pass the scrubby bushes half hidden on the skyline. (Depending on the state of cultivation, it may prove judicious to walk clockwise round the field boundaries, keeping them to your left.) A lovely panorama opens out as you reach the top of the hill and the bushes. In the top right corner go through a field gap and then walk forward to go through a wide double gate into the road.

**5.** Turn left. In a few yards continue straight ahead away from the road as it bends to the right. Walk through the field with a hedge on the left-hand side.

The way is now forward into the Cam valley again but first do enjoy the wonderful panorama. The valley comes into view as you then go down. Follow a right-angled bend. Again can be seen Wellow and St Julian's church but this time from a different angle.

The path goes steeply into a combe with St Julian's Well at its base. Keep the hedge on your left and go over three stiles. Cross the bottom of the combe, avoiding the marshy ground, and head towards the church along the waymarked grassy track on the far side.

Do not go through the gate but climb the stile immediately to the right. Walk along the edge of the field to reach the corner of the churchyard wall. Turn left over a stile to take you along the side of the wall (now on your right). It leads into a metalled track. After a few yards turn right into St Julian's churchyard and pass the church on your right-hand side.

**6.** The way leads to a raised causeway alongside the Wellow main street. Continue to the crossroads (the outward walk reached the village street here). Pass over the crossroads walking forwards as far as the Fox & Badger pub. Immediately turn left in front of the building and proceed down the cul-de-sac to the old disused railway line. Pass over it by the former signal box and continue down the enclosed pathway. Rather more than halfway down the steep hill, turn right by the second electricity pole and go over a stile.

**7.** A path now goes out of the village and down past the gardens to the fields bordering the meandering Cam brook. With the water on your left, walk through three fields and over two stiles. You mainly follow the water left, except where the track moves right and there is a brief stiled excursion through a spinney. Towards the end of the last very large meadow, you will be aware that the lane is closing in under the hill slope towards the brook and you. A third stile will bring you into the lane. Turn left. This pleasant lane will take you back to the starting point of the walk. To the left (viewed over a white gate) on the hillside lies the long barrow.

*Refreshments:* The Fox & Badger at Wellow serves a wide choice of dishes, both lunchtime and evening. There is also a village shop though this is closed Wednesday and Saturday afternoons and all day Sunday.

## NOTES

**Stony Littleton Long Barrow** dates back to about 2,500 BC and marks the start of man's occupation and taming of the natural landscape in these parts. These chambered barrows were family graves and were repeatedly opened up for the interment of elders. Ever since those times, important people have been venerated in some form of structure or death house, though now they are called mausoleums.

**The Somerset & Dorset Railway** (1862–1966) must have been welcomed by the villagers of Wellow, as the trains brought the world nearer to the isolated community. The Cam valley was not a previously undisturbed place though, for the rail track used much of the towpath of the failed arm of the Somerset Coal

Canal between Radstock and the River Avon. The Somerset &
Dorset is remembered with nostalgia for its many curves and
changes of gradient which contributed to its very pleasant
route. But it was also looked upon as a despoiler of the
countryside, and Wellow villagers are reconciled to the line
being axed. In some places the track has either been utilized for
farm access purposes or has completely disappeared. Only
occasionally does it exist as a visual feature, as at the eastern end
of the village where the viaduct overlooks the road.

# HAWKESBURY UPTON AND THE SOMERSET MONUMENT

*Hawkesbury church*

From Hawkesbury Upton, on the edge of the Cotswolds, where the hills roll themselves into long fingers before getting lost in the flat country to the west, there is some excellent walking country. Here is an outing of the very best which goes all round the Somerset Monument. The Prospect Tower, one of three all within 15 miles of each other, serves as a landscape feature and commands a very wide area. It was meant to be looked at, and from, and was built in 1846 as a memorial to General Robert Edward H Somerset (1776–1842), better known as Lord Edward Somerset. In the Waterloo campaign he commanded the Household Brigade of Cavalry and, as co-leader of the charge of the brigade, received particular mention in Wellington's despatches. The Beaufort family, of which he was a member, saw fit to commemorate his remarkable life with the Somerset Monument. It is not at present open to the public.

- **HOW TO GET THERE:** Hawkesbury Upton lies on the extreme north-easterly edge of the former county of Avon and may be approached from the A46 Bath/Nailsworth road 4 miles to the north of Old Sodbury. There is a car park next to the village hall, almost opposite to the Duke of Beaufort Arms.
- **LENGTH OF THE WALK:** 5 miles, which will take some 2 to 3 hours. Maps: OS Landranger 172 Bristol & Bath or OS Explorer 167 Thornbury, Dursley & Yate (GR 777870).

THE WALK

**1.** From the car park turn right along the main street. Pass Beaufort House (a home for the elderly) and turn left immediately before Hewetts Place. Take the right-hand of two tracks that leads to the waterworks reservoir. Follow the path that continues by the right side of the reservoir, and then follows a hedge on the right. Walk straight over the cross track and continue over a stile along the right-hand hedge down through a further two fields. There is a very fine view of the Somerset Monument on the right.

In the third field bear left down the hill to a stile in the dip on the wood's edge. Go over the stile and down through the tall mixed woodland to Hawkesbury, which stands under the hill. Well-clipped yew trees surround the large church with a tower and diminutive spire.

**2.** Pass by the church and immediately turn right into a gated metalled lane, a bridleway, unfenced at first. It passes under Hawkesbury Knott where there are signs of medieval strip lynchets, looking like giant footsteps on the hillside.

There are extensive views to the left over Inglestone Common and the green vale of Gloucester, with the distant rising hills of Wales on the far horizon. After about $^3/_4$ mile and

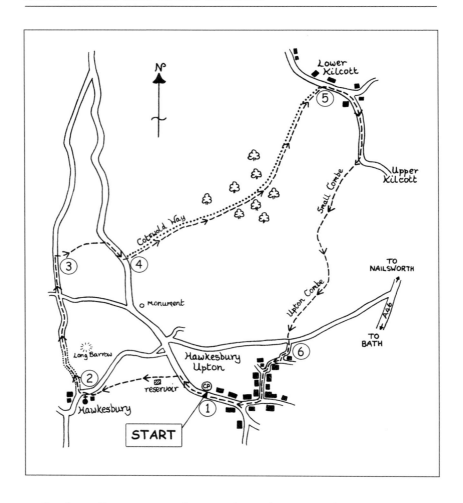

a further farm gate, the neglected pretty lane rises to a crossroads. Go straight over (northwards).

All around are more attractive clear views – Wickwar to the left, Wotton-under-Edge straight forward with Nibley Monument on the spur of the hill nearby. Behind lies the Stone Age long barrow on Hawkesbury Knott.

**3.** Very soon, at opposing stiles, take the double one on the right. Walk up the field towards the hill where another stile is in full view. Climb over this and then yet another almost immediately afterwards on the bank. Turn left and follow the fenced tall hedge on the left, which leads you steadily up the hill to the field corner at the top and a hunting gate. Turn right to resume your direction for a few yards to a gate into the road. Turn right along the road for about $1/4$ mile to reach the Cotswold Way long distance footpath. A superb view of the Somerset Monument is ahead. The interesting profile of Chinese influence dwarfs its surrounding trees.

**4.** At the signpost, turn away left into a track and follow the Cotswold Way by going through the gate facing the road. (Ignore the two tracks to the left.) Go straight across two very large pastures to the bottom left field corner of the final field. Pass through the field gate into the wood. Ignoring any tracks to your left, resume your direction immediately by walking along a waymarked broad stony track into the wood. After another one-third of a mile, the well-worn path ends at a wooden gate and

*The Somerset Monument*

stile. Pass into a pleasant meadow. Resume your direction with a hedge on the right to the meadow corner. Here turn left into a gated stony track which will take you downhill to the lane in Kilcot valley.

**5.** Leave the Cotswold Way by turning right along the lane. This is Lower Kilcot, consisting of one or two buildings and a mill and farm converted into very handsome dwelling houses. At the junction in the lanes keep right. Continue past a pumping station on the right. In something under $1/4$ mile just before the lane bends to the left and near to the vehicle passing place, turn right into Small Combe. It is a pleasant glade-like valley lined with woodland. The combe is used for pheasant breeding at certain times of the year.

After one-third of a mile, at a distinct division in the valley, go left. This arm becomes very narrow. There is a stream on the left at first that then wanders over to your right. Pass through the gate with stile. Follow the stream as the valley winds gently uphill. After a right bend where another stream comes in on the left, and where the trees fall away, continue to follow the bottom of the valley. Turn left over a wooden footbridge over the stream. Head upwards and right a short distance, to the gate in the top corner of the field. Continue forwards to the next gate, meantime rising up out of the valley. Go through a third gate.

Beyond the head of the valley on the right lies Hawkesbury Upton and there is another good view of the Monument from yet a different angle. The way up is now defined on the ground and it steepens as it nears the road (out of sight on the left). Go through the last gate up a short enclosed track to reach the road at a junction.

**6.** Cross straight over, and then follow the lane into Hawkesbury Upton. At the junction by the war memorial turn right into the main street. Pass the Fox Inn on the right. The car park, where the walk commenced, is also on the right.

*Refreshments:* The Duke of Beaufort Arms and the Fox in Hawkesbury Upton village. There is also a village shop.

NOTES

**Hawkesbury:** When the *Domesday Book* was written in the 11th century, Hawkesbury possessed woodland of two leagues wide and one league long. A prosperous village grew with a large church to serve the people and it also included Hawkesbury Upton one mile away. It is understood that although Hawkesbury Upton was granted a charter for a market the village never flourished because of lack of water, until, that is, the 19th century when a piped supply was made available. The village then came into its own and today it includes all the amenities that we expect of a thriving community.

What it does not possess though is an old church. For the latter we must turn to Hawkesbury under the hill about a mile away. Today's building is kept in mint condition and is a credit to the people who care for it and keep the surroundings so neat. The chancel is quite modest compared with the nave for it seems that the ecclesiastical patron who owned the chancel was reluctant to spend on a rebuild to match the lavish structure erected by the parishioners who were responsible for the nave.

# BERKELEY
# AND WHITCLIFF DEER PARK

*Berkeley Castle*

Berkeley lies in Gloucestershire, just beyond what was Avon's boundary, but the opportunity for a rewarding walk combined perhaps with a visit to one of England's finest inhabited castles is not to be missed. Whitcliff Park to the south of Berkeley is a long hog's back of a hill in the midst of a rich agricultural vale. It is often overlooked by the casual visitor, which is all the more reason to make the park 'a must'. Part of the walk goes through attractive farmland and the rest is over the hilly land of the grange where deer live in a traditional parkland setting.

- **HOW TO GET THERE:** By car – Berkeley lies on the B4066, 2 miles west of the A38 Bristol/Gloucester road. There is a free car park in Marybrook Street (near the library and school).
- **LENGTH OF THE WALK:** 6 miles, allow about 3 to 3$^1/_2$ hours. Maps: OS Landranger 162 Gloucester & Forest of Dean or OS Explorer 167 Thornbury, Dursley & Yate (GR 685993).

## THE WALK

**1.** From the centre of Berkeley, walk along the High Street (signposted Jenner Museum/St Mary's church). Pass the parish church with its detached belfry, the entrance to the Dr Edward Jenner museum, and the western side of Berkeley Castle. Follow the road for about $^3/_4$ mile through the hamlet of Ham passing the Salutation pub and the neat village green, with its red telephone box. Pass a road junction to Clapton and Bevington, enter a gate ahead immediately to the left of the junction, and follow a clear path towards the deer park. A wooden step stile in a brick wall will take you into the park.

**2.** Follow the chain-link and wooden fence for a short distance and then join the track. The way goes uphill and then out with good views on each side, including Tyndale's monument crowning Nibley Knoll, nine miles to the east. There is a waymark and then a fine line of horse chestnuts and lime trees ahead, which you will pass on your right-hand side. As you walk over the open ground, look for deer; they are to be seen in large numbers and include both red and fallow deer. As the line of trees comes to an end, look to your right to see Park House, still a dwelling. The park is upwards of 2 miles long. At the far end climb the wooden step stile in the brick wall. Pass through a field gate opposite into the field.

**3.** Turn right. Pass the lodge and follow the wall and hedge of the deer park on your right. Where the deer park wall falls away, continue along the hedge to a gate. Go through and resume your direction where there are rough tracks downhill to a gate into a farmyard. Walk through the farmyard and through a gate into a

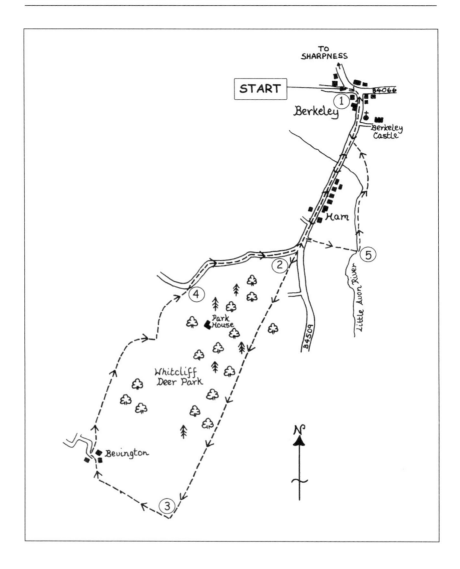

lane. There are brick cottages left and right of you. Immediately on the right and by the brick cottage, go through a waymarked iron gate. The guidepost is hidden in brambles and is difficult to see.

From here, cross a small paddock to a stile. Follow the right-hand hedge for a few yards when you will be able to see the next stile opposite. Climb the stile then turn and follow the left-hand hedge to the field corner where there is a stile and footbridge over a ditch, half hidden. This section of the route is little used, so take special care. The path goes through a tiny spinney to a further stile; again, special care. Follow the left-hand hedge to another stile in the corner. Cross the field (slightly left) to a field gate. Turn right into a farm lane.

Follow the lane for a short distance and, just before the farm, go through a gate on the left. Walk up the hill following the right-hand hedge. From the gate at the top the way goes down half right through a large sloping field to the road below. There are some excellent views after crossing the brow of the hill. Leave the field by the gate at the bottom right corner. (There is a sharp bend in the road at this point.)

**4.** Turn right into the road and follow it for about 1 mile until it meets the B4509 coming in from the right. You are now back at the hamlet of Ham at the point where you entered the deer park. Beyond the junction take a 'no through road' to the right, on the right of the village green leading to Brownsmill Farm.

**5.** Cross the bridge over the Little Avon and turn left along the riverbank. Berkeley Castle shows up clearly ahead, dominating the town. Follow the river until you see (but not cross) a second bridge from where you walk diagonally left across the field between the river and the castle grounds. Go over a stile by a stream to take you into the road. Turn right to reach the starting point.

*Refreshments:* Available in Berkeley and Ham. Berkeley is very quiet on Sundays. The Salutation and the Malt House (which is adjacent to the suggested car park) both offer lunch and evening meals (except Monday lunchtime) and available out of hours if pre-booked. The Malt House offers only a carvery menu at lunchtime on Sunday.

## NOTES
**Berkeley** is a small town with a spacious main street lined with buildings, most of them 18th century. Berkeley Castle has been

*Berkeley power station can be seen from the walk*

romantically described as rose and grey, the colour of old brocade. It dates from a shell keep and bailey of the 11th century but the main body is 14th century. It was in the reign of Henry II that Robert Fitzharding of Bristol built the first fortress to guard the vale, and it was here that Edward II was brutally murdered in 1307.

**Park House** is a castellated eye-catcher in Whitcliff Park, of early 19th century date. It is passed on the walk. Park lodges on the B4509 to Ham are similar in style but built a little later. They serve as kennels and offices.

**Edward Jenner**, born in 1749, practised as a country doctor. In 1796 he successfully proved to the world at large that by cowpox vaccination the dreadful smallpox scourge could be overcome. He died at the age of 72, and the east window of Berkeley church was re-fashioned in 1843 as a memorial.

**Whitcliff Deer Park** is one of the many which were granted throughout the country by the Crown, mainly during the 13th and 14th centuries. Wealthy feudal landlords, including the Church, used them for hunting the deer and lesser animals of the chase. In addition, the parks acted as animal ranches for the supply of fresh meat. The enclosing boundary first consisted of a high bank topped with a wood fence. There were leap gates at intervals, which allowed large animals such as deer free access. The parks were usually attached to a fortified stronghold, or, later, a great house. Some in the holding of a religious body had a farm or grange. By the 18th century many parks were landscaped and became cherished as suitable surroundings for their owners - people of privilege and social standing.

# CLEVEDON
# AND THE GORDANO VALLEY

*The pier and beach*

Seaside and coastal downs make an exhilarating outing. Here are both and, on a fine day, the views over the Bristol Channel towards the far away hills of Wales are enchanting. The walk climbs over Walton Down where the inland scene is equally attractive with the distant Mendips as a backcloth. The Gordano Valley makes a bold contrast to the woods and downs as it consists of a peaty wetland, which was drained and turned into a rich agricultural wedge between the areas of downland in the 19th century. The walk follows the side of part of the moor that has been preserved for its natural values.

- **HOW TO GET THERE:** By bus – there is an hourly bus service every day from Bristol to the Triangle. There is also an occasional local service to Bay Road, not Sundays. By car – from Bristol take the A369 Portishead road. Two miles beyond the flyover at the M6 Gordano interchange turn left on to the B3124 Clevedon road. One mile after passing Walton-in-Gordano, turn right to Walton St Mary. Park in Bay Road, opposite to the church of St Mary.
- **LENGTH OF THE WALK:** $4^1/_2$ miles; allow about $2^1/_2$ to 3 hours. Maps: OS Landranger 172 Bristol & Bath or OS Explorer 154 Bristol West & Portishead (GR 409727).

## THE WALK

**1.** Go down Bay Road and take the short flight of steps downwards to the left. Pass the public toilets, and then turn right along the coastal path (with the sea on the left). Pass steep steps down to Ladye Bay beach. The path begins to climb with tree and bush obscuring the sky – take care; some of the branches are quite low and can catch the head of the unwary. Once through the woods, there are extensive views of the attractive coastline with South Wales on the sea horizon. The well-walked path undulates along the extreme edge of the broken cliffs between gorse and scrub. Stunted bushes lean crazily in a struggle for survival against the prevailing wind from the Bristol Channel. Down below the seaweed strewn rocks attract many sea birds.

In $1^1/_4$ miles, having just passed (or stopped at) Roger's Seat, where the first housing can just be seen since leaving Clevedon, close to the trees there is a waymarked stile to the right. Climb this to take you on to the open down. Keep the hedge to your left as you climb the hill to reach a short lane and then come out into the road at the top.

**2.** Turn right. Walk for several hundred yards along the road. Take a narrow trackway on the left just before a road sign and Hill Cottage. It goes steeply up through a small spinney, then forks left and almost immediately left again. The way is steeply up the open ground to your left to the top of the down with the hedge to your left. There is then a faint path, which eventually

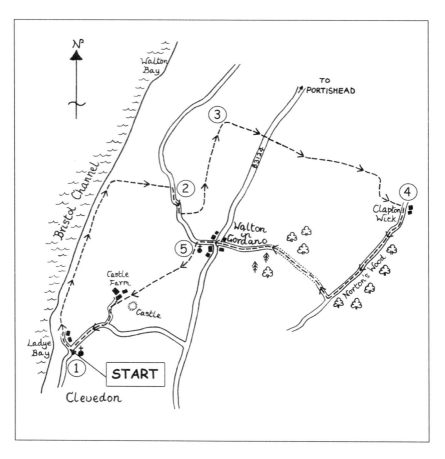

leads into a wood of small oaks. If you pause and turn, behind you is a most excellent vista of the Gordano Valley you are shortly about to cross. Enter the wood briefly by a narrow path, before passing into a clearing with fine views back towards the sea. The path bends to the right; keep the trees close to your left. Leave the clearing and enter a wood where the path now widens into a track, (observe a notice high on a tree on the left of the track) and after about 700 yards ends at a T-junction.

**3.** Turn right and go down the hill along the edge of a wood. Follow the path out of the wood to reach the Clevedon/Weston-in-Gordano road (B3124) below.

Cross straight over. Walk across the flat moor via a number of stiles to a wood, which you will see in the distance on your right (one third of a mile). The path enters the scrubby woodland by a double stile with a footbridge over the water channel (rhine). Continue forward by the side of the wood, which forms the eastern edge of Walton Moor, a wet peatland conservation area. At the end of the wood, go forward – this part of the walk might be boggy in wet weather – passing through a tall reed bed. Maintain the rhine just to your left. You will discover an exit stile in the left corner of the reed bed next to the rhine. The path leads to Clapton Wick but, before reaching the lane, there is first a right turn along a rhine and then a left turn over a double stile.

**4.** At the lane turn right (Clapton Wick Farm) and walk for upwards of $^3/_4$ mile to a junction. Turn right into Harley Lane leading into Moor Lane, which will take you across the vale to

*Church of St Paul, Walton-in-Gordano*

Walton-in-Gordano ($^3/_4$ mile). At the crossroads go straight over the B3124. After a few yards look for the entrance to St Paul's church.

**5.** Turn left into the neat churchyard and walk to the path beyond. Pass through a swing gate and paling fencing to gradually climb the hill. There is a pine wood to the right and cypresses to the left. A swing gate leads into an open space with wire fencing. A clear path goes forward and leads to a wide track through a neglected wood, which will take you to the top of the hill and a golf course. Keep to the track which then crosses a fairway (beware of golf balls). Enter the gated wood opposite and, as you leave this wood, on your left is Walton Castle. The way becomes tarred as it nears Castle Farm, with the golf course to your right. Continue forward passing the clubhouse and some houses on your right. Then the public highway comes into view. To reach Bay Road and your car, turn right along the road for about 400 yards.

*Refreshments:* The White Hart in Walton-in-Gordano is open every day and all day on Friday, Saturday and Sunday.

## NOTES

**Clevedon** is a modest seaside resort compared with busy Weston-super-Mare nearby. It was a tiny village at the beginning of the 1800s but the arrival of the railway caused it to expand on to the flat land to the east and this was facilitated by enclosure and by drainage of the peat moor. It tends to be overlooked that moors can be low lying marshy tracts as well as high heathy places. Whilst in Clevedon, consider visiting the pier and the Heritage Centre on the sea front.

**Gordano** is a strange and curious name. There have been guesses as to its derivation – perhaps the most plausible is that of a small wedge-shaped valley (gore) combined with the Old English 'dene'. Walton-in-Gordano's position by the side of the moor beneath the down keeps it sheltered from the sea gales. The 19th century church forms a focal point for the small village. Octagonal Walton Castle is of early 17th century date and was designed as a hunting lodge in Gothic style for Lord John Poulet of Hinton St George in Somerset. A few years ago it was a dangerous ruin with crumbling masonry but it has recently been rebuilt as a private dwelling house. There is a curtain of castellated walling which hides most of the building from public view.

**Clevedon Manor** (National Trust), 2 miles east of Clevedon, is a pleasant place to visit not only for its architecture, its portraits, and its Nailsea glass collection but also for its gardens and unostentatious atmosphere. Parts of the building are of 14th century vintage with Tudor additions and 18th century features.

*WALK 8*

# LANSDOWN, LANGRIDGE AND BATTLEFIELDS

❦

*The hamlet of Tadwick*

Battlefields gets its name from the military skirmish fought here during the Civil War (1643) between the Parliamentarians and the Royalists. The Parliamentarian force had the advantage of a hilltop position yet failed to rout the Cavaliers and the action ended in a stalemate. This peaceful walk takes you through the lovely countryside in which the action was fought. The downland was then a sheep grazing area and a prosperous one too, judging by the stone farmhouses of lasting quality which remain to this day and which have been adapted to a 21st century lifestyle.

- **HOW TO GET THERE:** By car – Lansdown Hill is 3 miles north of Bath on an unclassified road between Bath and the A420 Bristol road at Wick. Park in the lay-by adjacent to the lane to Langridge hamlet, $^3/_4$ mile north of Bath racecourse.
- **LENGTH OF THE WALK:** A hilly 5 miles, so allow 2 to 3 hours. Maps: OS Landranger 172 Bristol & Bath or OS Explorer 155 Bristol & Bath, Keynsham & Marshfield (GR.724691).

## THE WALK

**1.** From Lansdown Hill, turn into the lane leading to Langridge. It is a pretty lane which goes downhill by the side of a combe and ends in the larger valley running in a north/south direction to the Avon valley. On the left Langridge church of St Mary Magdalene stands in an elevated position above the lane.

**2.** After a mile, as the road starts to rise, take the first turn on the left before Tyning Cottage. It is a steep narrow lane lined with tall trees and so little used that a grass strip has grown along the middle. The track levels out. You pass a weather-boarded building and stone barn on the right. Before the track bends to the left and becomes a gated track, turn right immediately past the barn through an iron gate (waymarked) with squeeze through stile. The path contours the western side of the valley and passes below Manor Farm. At first it follows an iron fence and then walling. Across the valley is the hamlet of Tadwick in a most attractive setting. Ahead lies a delightful panorama of rising green fields topped by a screen of trees on Freezing Hill on the skyline. Also in the distance is Hamswell House.

Go under the electricity wires and continue through three fields. The stiles are waymarked and plain to see. After Goudie's Farm (basically 17th century with additions and also a 20th century extension) keep up on the hillside. Do not drop downwards. Head towards the pointed spinney where, in the dip beneath, the next stile will be seen about halfway along the hedge. It has a footbridge on its far side to provide the way over the small stream in the gully. From here the footpath goes half right down to a concrete farm track. At the farm entrance and just before a ford, turn left steeply back up the hill following the

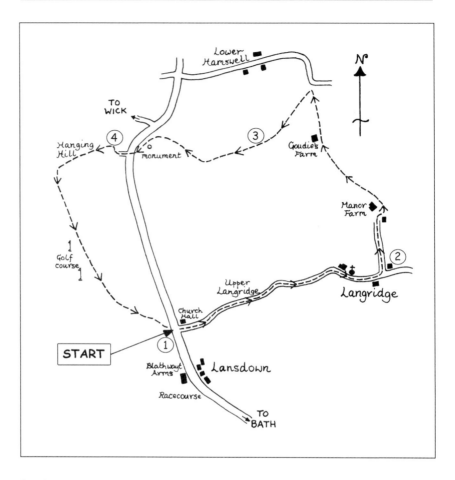

hedge on your right side to a stile in the corner joining you with
the Cotswold Way.

**3.** Continue forward from the stile. The path goes steeply uphill
in a southwesterly direction. Follow the waymarks. Towards the
top of the hill the footpath is defined on the ground and shows
the direction to take, passing a tree and bench seat on your
right. You may wish to sit and drink in the view. Two kissing
gates take you to a stony track.

On these slopes the Battle of Lansdown raged on one fateful
day in 1643. The downland was then well-grazed by sheep and

probably had less scrub as a result. Go through two swing-gates to reach a third and then a track. On the way notice a small copse planted in 1985 to the memory of Jack Cuff-Adams, a Cotswold Way warden.

Turn right along the good stony track, which is enclosed at first. Some 500 yards later, it becomes an open way after a metal gate. Bear right uphill at a fork. This narrow path leads to a restored stone stile with steps. Notice the newly completed restoration and information boards. Continue along the path through a field with walling on your right-hand side into a spinney. (Battlefields House may be seen through the trees on the right.) The path newly surfaced follows walling through the trees before ascending towards an open space. Climb a double stile to gain access to the monument of Sir Bevil Grenville, which stands at the end of an open field.

With your back to the monument, walk to the road (Lansdown Hill). Cross straight over along the signposted footpath. After a few yards it leads into a lane. Turn right towards the tall radio mast of the Observer Corps Early Warning station and Avon Fire Brigade HQ. Just before Sector Control entrance follow the lane which forks right.

After a few yards turn left to pick up a waymarked track (with yet another battle flag). The grassy way through the spinney soon peters out into a footpath. It leads through a new gate into open ground. Walk forward for about 500 yards and enjoy the superb view. From here, on the flat top of Hanging Hill, several landmarks may be identified on a clear day including the famous Clifton suspension bridge, Severn Bridge and the Second Severn Crossing. Straight ahead to the north in the middle distance lies Wick, whilst over to the west Bristol and its environs engulf the scene.

**4.** When the walling on your left ends, to be replaced by fencing, turn left through a new field gate. It is the beginning of a bridleway that will take you back to the starting point of the walk. On the way pass a wood (left) and walk alongside the Lansdown golf course (right). Continue forward. Pass over a metalled road and continue to the end of the wood and a junction. Continue forward along the bridleway. At the metalled road of the racecourse turn left over a stile and then fork right to reach Lansdown Hill and the start of the walk.

*Refreshments:* The Blathwayt Arms, Lansdown Hill, with a wide choice of menu.

## NOTES

**Lansdown** (long hill) is one of several finger-like spurs of the Cotswolds which end in the Avon valley. A large portion was purchased between 1690 and 1701 by William Blathwayt of Dyrham (Secretary of State to William and Mary). The Star Inn by the present racecourse then changed its name to the Blathwayt Arms. In the 19th century the horse races were run from Beckford's Tower to Lansdown Lane, but after 1830 the annual meeting was moved to its present position.

**William Beckford's Tower** (built 1827) is open to visitors at weekends (2 pm to 5 pm). This Italianate-style building has 154 stone steps to take you up to the top to admire the view. William Beckford (1760-1844) was a wealthy eccentric who inherited a fortune based on the North Jamaican sugar plantations. His reclusive declining years were spent in Bath. From his home in Lansdown Crescent he had a private landscaped drive to his tower, but today that has gone.

**Sir Bevil Grenville** was mortally wounded during the Battle of Lansdown and the monument of 1720 was set up by his grandson, Lord Lansdown. The family changed its name to Granville in the 17th century.

# NEWTON PARK
# AND STANTON PRIOR

❦

*The Globe Inn near Newton St Loe*

Newton St Loe stands on a bluff of land south-west of the River Avon near to Bath. It makes a good starting point for a short and pleasant walk which first goes through Newton Park, where there is a glimpse of the lake, which recently underwent clearing and re-landscaping and is popular with anglers. After rising gently upwards out of the valley the walk then passes under the eastern end of Stantonbury Hill before returning through Stanton Prior and a different way through Newton Park. For an energetic addition take the footpath to the top of Stantonbury (about 500 ft) – it will add one mile to the walk.

- **HOW TO GET THERE:** By bus – Bristol/Bath service X39, $^1/_4$-hourly every day, will stop at the Globe Inn. With the Globe Inn on your right pass the car park and go into the field by the roadside. Follow the clear path uphill (road on left) to Newton St Loe. Turn right into the road and right again to reach the church of Holy Trinity. By car – park near to Holy Trinity church, Newton St Loe. The approach to the village is near the junction of the A4 Bath/Bristol road with the A39 Marksbury Road at the Globe Inn.
- **LENGTH OF THE WALK:** 4 miles for car users and $5^1/_2$ miles for bus goers; an easy walk taking about $2^1/_2$ to 3 hours. Maps: OS Landranger 172 Bristol & Bath or OS Explorer 155 Bristol & Bath (GR 701649).

## THE WALK

**1.** At the entrance to the church, go through the churchyard, pass the porch, and out via the swing gate into the field

*Holy Trinity church, Newton St Loe*

beyond. There is a faint path downwards and slightly left to a wooden swing gate (garage on the left). Turn left down the gravelled cul-de-sac to reach the tarmac lane. Turn right. At the junction of two lanes continue forward (the left-hand one), along a new gravel path with a stream on the left, to an iron swing gate. Go across the road and into Newton Park College grounds by the opposite swing gate. On the right there is a good distant view of Corston.

Proceed along the grass track. Cross the stream and go over a stile and slightly uphill. The northern end of the lake is on the left with the college students' accommodation overlooking the water. Continue forward to the open ground ahead rising gently. Pass over a stile adjacent to two mature oaks on your left. Continue up the green vale with the stream on your left-hand side. High up on the right there has been a replanting of an old stretch of wood. At the top of the vale and over a stile pass a partly restored building on your left ('New Barn'). The path is plain to follow along the edge of a large cultivated field. Very soon it goes left over a stream at a field boundary and then along a hedge, again on your left, to the lane.

**2.** Turn left. This narrow lane leads to Stanton Prior ($^3/_4$ mile). The hill on your right is Stantonbury, which, as the name suggests, has an Iron Age hill fort on the top. It is linked with the linear earthwork called Wansdyke but the embankment here is so slight that it appears as an ordinary field boundary and can easily be missed. Taking a path through an en-crested gate on the right about $^1/_2$ mile after joining the lane to Stanton Prior, one may make a diversionary but gentle climb of Stantonbury Hill. The path is overgrown at first but improves after a while. Return to the lane afterwards.

As you approach the hamlet ignore the two right turns and pass Poplar Farm on your left. Continue to the small right turn; a blue road sign indicates a no through road. This way becomes decidedly narrower where you emerge into the lane opposite to the church of St Lawrence.

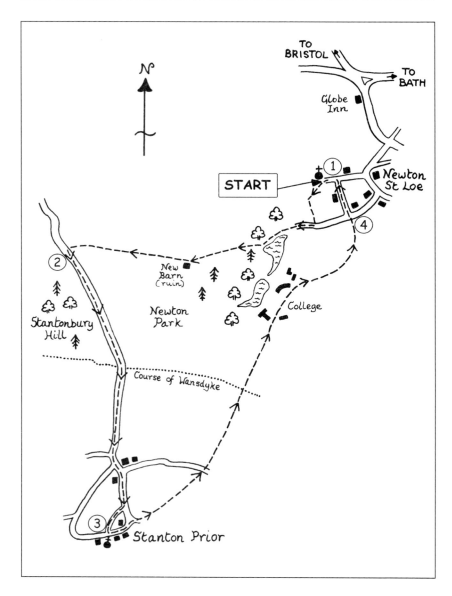

**3.** Turn left. To leave the quiet hamlet pass by the small Nonconformist chapel (now a dwelling) to the junction, where there is a stile. A waymarked path then leads half right through a cultivated field, then through a second field. The stile here is in the bottom right corner; exit to a narrow lane. Pass straight over by way of a stile and follow the right-hand hedge to the end of the next field where there is a footbridge and stile. Turn right into a slightly overgrown green track. Very soon it bends to the right before going slightly uphill and ends at a stile. Climb the stile into Newton Park. Walk the slope upwards keeping the hedge on your left.

Soon the distant buildings of the college may be seen, flanked by the pleasant green valley. Walk forwards and towards a distant electricity pole and pass over the stile and under the electricity wires, then cross the playing field walking down a newly planted avenue of trees and over the hard court towards the college buildings. The stile into the playing field is about halfway along the line of trees flanking the field.

The buildings consist of an old Jacobean range of farm housing with the older, 13th century keep and a modern college block. Aim just to the right of the modern block.

There is now a metalled drive to be followed passing first between new blocks bearing local names such as Newton and Corston, and then by the 18th century mansion house on the left. Continue by the Steward's lodge on your right-hand side and forward through an elaborate gate along the newly tree-lined avenue for a further $^1/_2$ mile to the entrance of the outer park.

**4.** Opposite is a lane that leads up to the cul-de-sac by the church and the starting point of the walk for car users. Bus users should turn right and then left to pick up the footpath back past the Globe Inn.

*Refreshments:* The Globe Inn near Newton St Loe on the A4 Bristol/Bath road.

**NOTES**
**Newton St Loe's** name is derived from its first Norman overlord, Geoffrey Bishop of Coutances and St Loe. He came to this country at the time of the Conquest and was a trustee of William I. His reward was a vast estate that he divided amongst his kin. Thus a branch of the St Loe family came and settled in the valley and the

previous Saxon village became Newton St Loe. Today there are several fine old farmhouses, one of which may be seen near to the church. It is called 'Stone Walls' and has a weathervane and an ammonite on its handsome front. Opposite lies the Free school of forward-looking Richard Jones of Stowey, who founded it in 1698 (when Free schools were set up they were not meant to be free in the monetary sense but the schooling provided was of a public and liberal nature). The William and Mary-style building (privately owned) is a good specimen of its period.

**Holy Trinity church** has the whole of the south side taken up by the Langton family pews. From the 18th century this family owned the village that served their mansion and the park. There is also a large monument surrounded by an early example of cast iron railings (previously all were hand wrought). Outside the porch may be seen an old scratch dial, which pre-dates clocks, by which the villagers could tell the time of church functions. Opposite is a good church cross set upon an ancient plinth.

**Newton Park** was purchased by Joseph Langton, a wealthy Bristol merchant who commissioned Launcelot (Capability) Brown to create a suitable setting for his new mansion house. The landscape gardener commands as much respect today as when he made his name in the 18th century with his parks containing long vistas, serpentine lakes, and carefully careless glades. To his credit he retained several old buildings in Newton Park, notably the restored range of Jacobean farmhouses and the 13th century keep. It is particularly good that the latter is still standing, as most of Avon area's really ancient strongholds have disappeared or been reduced to a few mounds of earth. There is a modern school block nearby. Several new blocks have been and are being added and it is these that have the names of local villages. All form part of the College of Further Education that occupies the park. Joseph Langton's rococo-style mansion also has a modern school block attached to it, which blends in tolerably well. The park's ground landlord is the Duchy of Cornwall; it was acquired in 1940. It is the Duchy's crest that you see on the gate to Stantonbury Hill.

**Stanton Prior** formed part of the estate of Bath Priory until its dissolution with the larger monasteries in the 16th century. St Lawrence's church is modest in size. It contains much 19th century work but has several older portions. Outside in the graveyard stands a yew tree which suffered badly in the winter gales of recent years. Efforts have been made to limit the damage caused and now only time will tell whether the decapitation of the upper section will save the tree. Legend has it that there was once a plague pit near to the church and a gravedigger discovered a number of skeletons under the roots of the yew.

**Wansdyke** is an Iron Age earthwork of the post Roman period. Doubt has been expressed as to where it started and went to, but now it is generally accepted that it ran from the Bristol Channel into the Savernake Forest. Likewise little is known of its purpose save that it was a marker of territorial ownership. To trespass was to risk the loss of an ear or some other gruesome punishment.

# BLAGDON LAKE
# AND FELTON COMMON

*Blagdon Lake*

Felton Common, the largest common south of Bristol, makes a perfect starting place for a walk. Downwards wends the way to the Yeo valley where Blagdon Lake, with its still waters, lies in an idyllic setting. This is a comparatively little frequented area which contains a patchwork of narrow lanes and attractive bridleways. There are few villages and therefore there is little traffic to disturb the peace.

- **HOW TO GET THERE:** By car – Lulsgate Bottom is near to Bristol Airport on the A38 Bristol/Burnham on Sea road. Park opposite St Catherine's church, Felton Common, in

West Lane. The walk begins at the church. By bus – there is an hourly weekday service, Bristol/Weston-super-Mare, via the airport. Alight at Lulsgate Bottom and turn back towards Bristol. Turn right into West Lane (signposted Winford) and right again to enter Felton Common near St Catherine's church. There is also a 20-minute service to the airport from Bristol bus station; this does not stop on the main road.

- **LENGTH OF THE WALK:** $6^1/_2$ miles. Allow about 3 to $3^1/_2$ hours. Maps: OS Landranger 172 Bristol & Bath or OS Explorer 154 Bristol West & Portishead (GR.515656).

## THE WALK

**1.** From the church, take a track going diagonally right across the common towards a group of cottages. On reaching the cottages, keep the hedge on your right. The track passes a converted windmill on the right. The airport buildings can also be seen. Leave the common at its end (Felton Hill). Keep the hedge on your right, immediately pass a few farm buildings, right, and, after a couple more yards, take the right-hand unmarked bridleway. It is broad and pleasant and enclosed on both sides with hazel trees. Pass a farm called Hunter's Hall on the right and soon, at the junction, cross the road, signposted Butcombe. At the next crossroads go ahead keeping your southerly direction. Pass Row of Ashes Farm on your right. Soon there is a very good view ahead towards the wooded slopes of Mendip. At the Butcombe Brewery (Rusling House), fork right (but note that, at the time of writing, the brewery is scheduled to be moved – see Notes on page 74).

**2.** The road now goes downhill. When you reach the T-junction, you will see a beech tree planted in memory of RAF pilot J. C. Milliken who was killed in the Second World War. Take the right fork. After about 500 yards (at the top of a rise in the road) turn left into a bridleway, pleasant at first, but becoming steep and stony. It leads down towards Blagdon Lake, which soon comes into view. Beyond the lake lies Blagdon village, with its large church and 15th century tower set against the green Mendips.

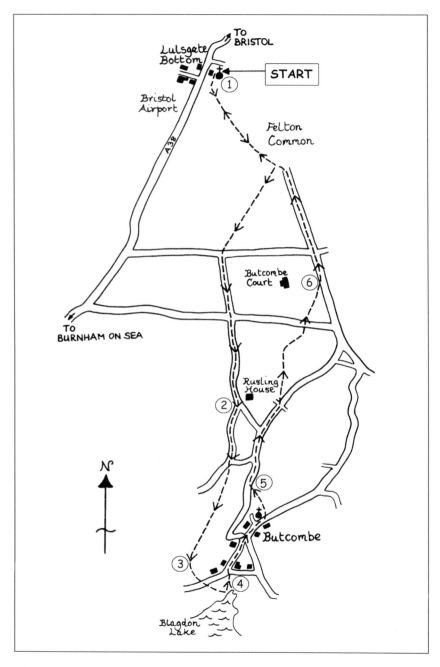

*The small and beautiful church at Butcombe*

Near at hand to the left, the small hamlet of Butcombe nestles into a fold of the rolling hillside.

**3.** The bridleway now goes downhill. When you reach the road, cross over and go through the left of two gates. Follow the right-hand hedge to a gap. Go through and then follow the left-hand hedge to the corner of the field where there is a stile.

A short diversion here of about $^1/_4$ mile (worth it if you have time; a place also to picnic) will take you along the northern shore of Blagdon Lake. For this diversion, turn right for a few yards, cross the stile and almost immediately climb over another stile on the right. The path passes very near to the lakeshore where it is extremely pleasant and sheltered. Return the same way and cross the stile in the field corner already mentioned to bring your direction northerly.

Follow the right-hand boundary of the wood along three fields and then through a gate, top right corner, into the road opposite Yew Tree Farm.

**4.** Turn right to Butcombe hamlet. Walk past a right turning and also where the Mill Inn once was. Keep right at the next fork, signposted 'Church and Village Hall', and go up the steep hill past the small and beautiful church on the left. Immediately after the church take a footpath through an iron swing gate. The short enclosed path leads to a stile and open ground. Keep to the top of the bank until a stream is reached, then drop downhill half-left to a stile and footbridge well concealed in the field bottom. Resume your direction and walk up the steep neglected field. The field is most uneven; take care. Pass the single oak tree. In the topmost corner of the field, go through a somewhat hidden corner gate into the road. Make your approach from close up to the right hedge.

**5.** Turn right. Continue uphill along the road and, at the junction opposite The Firs, turn right. Very soon and immediately after Cherry Tree Cottage, a cross junction of a track is reached.

Go through the faintly blue iron gate from the road into a field on the left. Continue half right across the large pasture towards the corrugated iron-roofed farm buildings, at first concealed. To the right of these buildings, go through another very faint blue iron gate. Immediately turn left to the corner of the field and climb the stone stile. Go forward where the next wooden stile will be seen on a high bank. This leans outwards and a little agility is required here. It is waymarked and points the direction. (Follow the right-hand hedge at first and leave it near to the farm buildings.) The next wooden stile is halfway along the wood and wire fence. It will take you into the entrance drive of Merry Hill Farm. Cross the road at the end of the drive. Half hidden in the hedge is a stile, which might be rather overgrown. You may wish to go on the walk prepared for this. Go through into a meadow. As you proceed diagonally half right you will see to the left of the farm buildings a metal farm gate and swing gate. You may prefer to use the farm gate. Continue half-right towards the lodge. (There is a row of very fine lime trees leading back to the Court.) In the right-hand corner of the meadow near to the lodge climb the iron step stile.

**6.** Turn left – this is Thrubwell Lane. When you reach the crossroads go straight over. After about 750 yards you will meet the point where you left Felton Common on the outward walk. Return to your car or the bus stop by the same route.

*Refreshments:* The Airport Tavern, Lulsgate Bottom and the George & Dragon at Felton.

NOTES

**Felton Common** consists of an open heath near to Lulsgate Bottom. It is the largest common still existing south of Bristol and it is of great appeal to many people. The undivided commons of old were used for summer grazing and formed a major feature of village life for hundreds of years; it was not until the 19th century that many disappeared. Overgrazing led to some becoming exhausted resulting in a reversion to poor pasture. As such they were then not sought after for enclosure in the 18th and 19th centuries. Those which still exist may be heath as at Felton, or scrub, wood or semi-wood, fen or moor.

**Lulsgate airport**, developed during the Second World War by the Air Ministry, was derelict when Bristol Corporation purchased it in 1955. It opened about two years later. Bristol Corporation failed to capitalize on their investment and it was sold on. Recently Bristol turned down the opportunity of its own airport at Filton, so changes were made to improve the passenger building at Lulsgate. Expansion has been threatened several times, which would encroach upon Felton Common, but to date all efforts to extend it have been fended off. Lulsgate Airport is now rather grandly titled Bristol International Airport.

**The Mendip Lake District** is a title given to the man-made lakes of Blagdon and Chew Valley. Before the 1900s Bristol's water was supplied from large tanks near to Barrow Gurney. Increasing demand led to the creation first of Blagdon Lake at the turn of the century and then, some 50 years later, of the Chew Valley lake. The river Yeo was dammed for Blagdon Lake and it is the northern end, called Butcombe Bay, which is featured in the walk. The stream entering at this point is one of the main feeders and the well-oxygenated water encourages the aquatic life upon which the fish feed. It is an internationally recognized trout fishery. Many farms in the catchment area have been provided with sewage disposal units to prevent contamination.

**Butcombe village** has lost its pub, post office and village shop, but St Michael's church, a short way up the hill, provides a good centre for the hamlet. The old Butcombe Brewery site, which started production in 1978 and is passed en route, keeps alive the tradition of the small local brewer who produces his own special ale, which is worth sampling. The brewery is moving from its present site, so let's hope that Butcombe doesn't lose its brewery too.

# BATHAMPTON DOWN AND THE KENNET AND AVON CANAL

*The Kennet and Avon Canal*

Bath is unique. And what better way of taking an elevated look at its classical outlines than by a walk up to the southern plateau. The Georgian facades can be seen layered upon the surrounding hill slopes. The nature of Bath's situation has kept urban sprawl within limits so that today it is still possible to walk through pleasing green surroundings and yet stay within the confines of the city. Do take this stroll from Bath Abbey in its very heart – you will find that road walking is minimal and the city approaches quiet and uncluttered by unsightly buildings. The climb upwards is steep but short. Bathampton Down is broad and open with exciting vistas. A gentle downward way leads to the Kennet and Avon Canal, which lies, slightly elevated, in the Avon valley. There is also a surprise to the walk with a pleasant way through two old established municipal parks.

- **HOW TO GET THERE:** By car – Bath Abbey lies in the centre of the city where there are several long-stay car parks. The nearest one to the abbey is North Parade Road Leisure Centre parking area. It lies on the eastern side of the River Avon and is marked on the sketch plan. Consider the park and ride schemes at Newbridge and Lansdown. Currently it is possible to park in Victoria Park on Sundays at no charge. By bus – from the bus station approach Bath Abbey along Manvers Street.
- **LENGTH OF THE WALK:** $4^{1}/_{2}$ miles; about $2^{1}/_{2}$ hours. Maps: OS Landranger 172 Bristol & Bath or OS Explorer 155 Bristol & Bath (GR 753647).

**THE WALK**

**1.** Leave the eastern end of Bath Abbey and go towards the river by walking past Orange Grove, with its obelisk and circular garden traffic island. Turn right along Grand Parade, with the sunken Parade Gardens on your left. Turn left at the traffic lights into North Parade. Pass over the Avon and pause to enjoy the delightful prospect of sparkling waters, the U-shaped weir and the elegant Palladian-style structure bridging the Avon. Continue to the T-junction with Pulteney Road.

**2.** Pass the toilets on your right and cross over and go through the railway archway between the two green road signs to reach the Kennet and Avon Canal up the steps. At the canal, turn right along the towpath past the canal lock. Immediately afterwards, turn left over the pretty wrought-iron footbridge. Ahead lies a steep upward path, then a road and two flights of steps. At the top, with a field on your right, continue up to a right-hand bend in the path. Here turn left to reach Bathwick Hill, and cross straight over into Cleveland Walk. Go along this quiet road for $^{1}/_{4}$ mile. Opposite Sham Castle Lane, look for a narrow footpath between tall walls which will take you up to North Road and a splendid view.

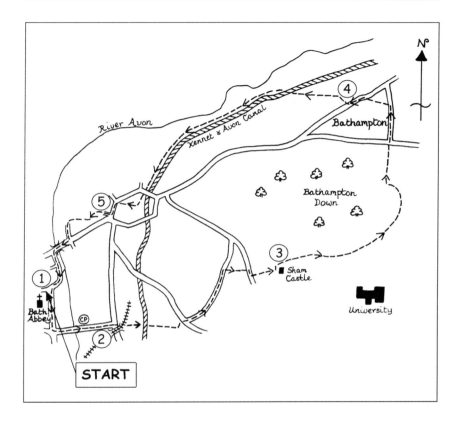

Turn right along North Road for about 75 yards, then cross over and climb the steps and stile into a steeply sloping area of neglected scrub and bushes. The footpath through this National Trust field (North Road Meadows) will take you up to Sham Castle folly. Halfway up, cross over the entrance drive of the golf course. The folly, situated on open ground, will suddenly come into view through a spinney. Here you will want to pause for a breather and take in the panorama of Bath, cradled by hills.

**3.** Turn left and immediately right (before the golf clubhouse). A track, going gently upwards, takes you towards the trees. There is walling and a barbed wire fence on your right-hand side. Follow this and, at a waymark post where the path forks, continue forward over the last yard or so of metalled path.

Follow the waymarks directing you to a fingerpost and here turn right. Continue forward (waymarked) to reach a spinney enclosing a path, turn left and the rear of Bath University will be on your right.

Bathampton Down now lies ahead, with its open and agreeable space suitably landscaped with many kinds of young trees. At the blue waymarked cross tracks, continue forward for upwards of a third of a mile to reach the edge of the scarp.

At a waymarked fork, just where there are three trees growing out from a small bank on the left, bear left (a permissive path), skirting the wood and small clearings on your right. When a low waymarked barbed wire fence is encountered turn right into the wood, down a few steps with a guide rail, and follow the track as it immediately swings round to the left. The track soon descends steeply.

At a waypost, turn right, noticing the fenced quarry to your left. This is the old stone quarry of Bathampton Rocks. Cross an iron stile and follow the path, which has a new barbed wire fence on the left. Go through the trees and a wooden kissing gate into open ground that slopes away to the right, with a rewarding view of the Avon valley. The Bath TV transmitter is straight ahead. Turn right when joining an at-first grassy, then steep and stony, downward track. Pass through a metal field gate to reach the housing on the western side of Bathampton and the A36 Bath/Warminster road. Your direction is still towards the bottom of the valley.

Cross over the main road into Down Lane, passing Devonshire Road on your left and, after about another 100 yards, look for a footpath sign (left) which leads you into a small new housing development (Miller Walk). The path exits the houses to the right of the last house via a kissing gate into a meadow. In the meadow, follow the path to the lower left corner that leads out into Bathampton Lane.

4. Turn left along the lane for about 50 yards. At the signpost, turn right along Candy's Path. This is a short track leading to pleasant pasture bordering the Kennet and Avon Canal. Turn left at the waymark and walk through the pasture. There is a lovely

vista of the outer environs of Bath and Little Solsbury Hill across the valley. The path closes with a gate to take you over the canal. After the bridge, turn left to reach the towpath.

Walk towards the city for about $^1/_2$ mile. Go under Beckford Road tunnel and then under an elegant footbridge with wrought-iron work. Before the second of these splendid footbridges, leave the canal by turning right into Sydney Gardens. This is a quiet haven, with many tall, mature, deciduous trees. Follow the broad avenue over the railway and continue down past the Roman Temple to the main entrance gates. Cross the busy road near the junction and turn left along Sydney Place.

**5.** Opposite the Holburne of Menstrie museum, turn right into Sutton Street. Pass the Pulteney Arms public house and enter Henrietta Gardens. The footpath is between Henrietta Mews and Henrietta Gardens. Keeping to the left-hand side of the park, follow the tarred way past the public toilets to the far side of the gardens and the Henrietta Street exit. (The attractive memorial garden is at this exit.) Turn left into Henrietta Street, which will take you to the road junction called Laura Place. Turn right into Argyle Street. Pass over the Pulteney Bridge with its tiny shops. Turn left along Grand Parade, which will take you back to the starting place by Bath Abbey.

*Refreshments:* There is a tea house in the grounds of the Holburne of Menstrie museum serving very adequate pots of tea, home-made cakes, and hot and cold lunches (but not Mondays). There are also ample pubs and restaurants in Bath itself.

### NOTES
**Sham Castle** is an empty facade built of stone from Bathampton Down. It was constructed for the pleasure of Ralph Allen, of Prior Park, in 1762, a couple of years before his death. Its appearance of castellated towers flanking a gateway has a certain romantic appeal as an eye-catcher. At night it is floodlit.

**Bathampton Down** overlooks the fertile Avon valley and its trio of attractive villages of Bathampton, Batheaston and

*Sham Castle*

Bathford. Their close proximity to the city of Bath with its attendant urban spread has put them in jeopardy of being absorbed and they keenly maintain their individual characters. On the down many ancient features, notably an Iron Age camp and field system, may be seen as the land was formerly a common, which has resulted in the remains being undisturbed by the plough.

**Bathampton Rocks** consists of hummocky ground of mines and quarries used for stone extraction. At the beginning of the 19th century, much of the stone used for the Kennet and Avon Canal came from here. Bath stone is a freestone, which means that it cuts easily in several directions. It is one of a series of Jurassic limestones, so called because the grains are tightly packed and resemble the roe of a fish.

**The Kennet and Avon Canal** is very popular with wild fowl and swans, not to mention the fishermen, walkers and leisure craft users. Engineered by John Rennie and opened in 1810, it was cut to take the traffic of heavy goods between Bristol and London via Reading and the River Thames. The walk first crosses the canal at the top of a short flight of locks that carries the water down to the Avon. It is met up with once more outside Bath in one of its fine quieter stretches where a flash of brilliant blue may be occasionally seen as the kingfisher skims low over the water. After passing the Beckford Road tunnel, the canal goes through Sydney Gardens, which had opened only a few years before the canal was cut. This is the reason for the pleasant footbridges that connect the gardens. They were referred to as 'Chinese' when they were set into position shortly after the turn of the 19th century. The canal was highly successful until 1841 when Brunel's Great Western Railway came through Bath and thereafter grabbed the heavy goods traffic. Today, the efforts of the Canal Trust to reopen it to pleasure craft are paying off and the canal is now both popular and viable.

**Henrietta Park** is relatively new in comparison with Sydney Gardens. It was donated by Captain F. W. Forester and opened in 1897. It contains a garden of remembrance dedicated to King George V (1936).

**Pulteney Bridge** was designed by Robert Adam and completed in 1774. Its purpose was to make the new town of Bathwick (then being built) accessible to the city, as previously the only passage was by means of a ferry.

# BLAISE CASTLE
# AND SEA MILLS

*Blaise Hamlet*

Although in the suburbs of Bristol, this is a splendid walk through green places and tree-lined footpaths away from the hurly-burly. For much of the time, it is also out of sight of the built-up areas. Many of the footpaths are metalled and so it is well suited to families with small children and accessible for folding pushchairs though there is a short, steep, stony assent to the castle. The way goes first through the small gorge of the River Trym down to the Avon estuary and returns via Kings Weston Hill and Blaise Castle estate.

- **HOW TO GET THERE:** By bus – there are frequent local services on weekdays to and around Henbury. We recommend City Bus Service X56/6 Colston Avenue. Walk to Kings Weston Road. By car – Blaise Castle is approximately 4 miles from the centre of Bristol. Take the A4018 Bristol to Cribbs Causeway road and fork left at Westbury-on-Trym to Henbury. There is a large free car park in Kings Weston Road on the northern side of Blaise Castle estate. From the parking area, walk along the right-hand side of Kings Weston Road towards Henbury village.
- **LENGTH OF THE WALK:** $4^1/_2$ miles, which will take about 2 to $2^1/_2$ hours. Maps: OS Landranger 172 Bristol & Bath, OS Explorer 155 Bristol & Bath, 154 Bristol West. (GR 555785)

## THE WALK

Note: At the junction of Kings Weston Road with Hallen Road, a National Trust sign indicates the way to Blaise Castle hamlet. Do take this interesting diversion either before or after the walk.

**1.** From Kings Weston Road, pass the entrance to Blaise Castle Folk Museum. Leave the main road and walk along Church Lane, turning right into Church Close with its pleasant 17th century buildings, to enter the churchyard of St Mary, Henbury. On the right-hand side of the church porch it is worthwhile looking for the burial place of Scipio Africanus, an African slave, who died in his teens and was interred there by his master in 1720. Walk past the church on your left-hand side to reach the far boundary of the churchyard where a short flight of steps leads down through a tunnel to reach the river Trym. Take care as the floor of the tunnel is slippery.

**2.** Cross the bridge and turn right with the water on your right-hand side. This extremely pleasant place has a good mix of trees, including weeping willows. Very soon Stratford Mill is passed on its reconstructed site (day visit centre). Pass over the track junction and continue along the broad metalled way through the wooded coombe. Keep the river on your right. The cliffs on

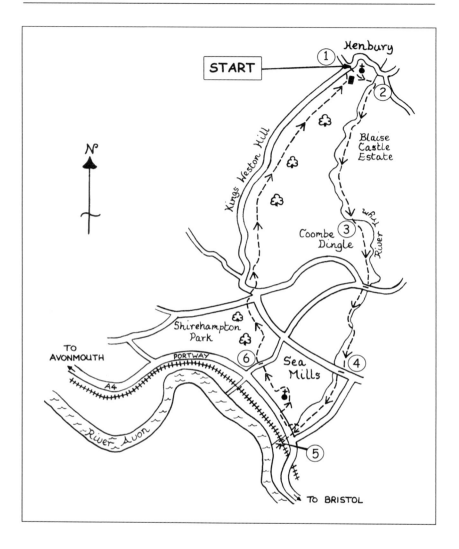

each side are impressively tall and show sheer limestone faces in places.

Walk through the gorge and ignore any bridges and cross ways until after passing an oval-shaped pond. The broad track swings to the left and gently rises. Continue on this broad path looking down to the stream on your right. When the track returns to river level, there is a small cliff on the left and a small stone footbridge on the right. Ignore this and proceed forward with the river still on the right.

**3.** At the next and last footbridge, cross the river so that it now flows on your left. The gorge is left behind as the vale broadens and goes through Coombe Dingle. Continue through a neat car park until the metalled road is reached (The Dingle). Turn right along the road. After two or three yards, turn left through the second of two gaps in the fence on your left, and continue your original direction along a concreted-over pipe. Pass under Dingle road bridge and then walk through a broad green area close to the river. Cross the river at the next footbridge and follow the path with the water now on your right to Sea Mills village. The road is reached at the rear of an inn called the Mill House.

**4.** Turn right and pass in front of the inn. Cross the road and, in a few yards, pick up a narrow path through a gap on your left (with the river on your right-hand side again). This earthen way opens out into a long grassy recreation ground where there is a row of fine young poplars lining the water's edge. Cross the metalled road ahead and continue towards the distant six-arched road bridge of the Bristol Portway. Presently, on your left, is Sea Mills Lane. Pass under the bridge to view the remains of the old harbour of Sea Mills (originally the Roman port of Abonae).

**5.** Walk over the railway level crossing to reach the Avon at the point where the River Trym flows into the estuary. The mud banks attract many interesting birds, particularly waders. Here, before the Avon signal station, the ships waited for the tide to take them into Bristol harbour. It is a very pleasant spot, with a good view towards Shirehampton and passing shipping on the tide.

Retrace your steps under Portway bridge and cross the Trym by the footbridge on your left. Bear left at the junction of paths to reach the main road. Turn right onto the Bristol Portway and right again into Riverleaze. This road through the housing estate bends to the left and passes St Edyth's church. Turn left into

Avonleaze and right to join a little used footpath between the houses. Go straight on at the right fork where the path enters a wood. You will be aware that the Bristol Portway is a short distance away to your left. Continue along the side of the wood, at the end of which you come out on a road.

**6.** Cross straight over into Shirehampton Park (golf course). Turn right and walk uphill near to the right-hand boundary and road. The view back over your left shoulder is a very fine one as the whole of the wide horseshoe bend of the Avon comes into view. Leigh Woods in the far distance form an interesting backcloth.

In the top corner of the park go through a swing gate and cross the road. Turn right past Park Lodge towards the road junction. Continue left round the side of Park Lodge. Cross the Kings Weston Road near to the junction into a metalled path opposite. It goes uphill and parallel with the Kings Weston Road for a short distance. At a junction in the path, near to a footbridge, turn right. A wide track then leads up to the top of Kings Weston Hill and passes the television mast on your right. Before the mast, the track forks to form two paths roughly parallel with each other. Take the grassy left-most path, since the right stony track is a bridleway. Our path is a broad grassy way that goes along the flat summit of the down for about $1/2$ mile. There are mature trees bordering each side. The left and right tracks converge near a cross track, but continue forward. The path narrows at the end. Enter the trees on the left-hand side by a swing gate.

Through the mixed woodland the path then goes down steeply to the corner of a large, open, grassy recreation area in Blaise Castle estate. Maintain the same direction and soon enter the wood again. Take the broader stony ascending path and climb up to the triangular castle-like tower on top of the grassy down. This is Blaise Castle folly. As you pass by, it is worthwhile turning right to the viewpoint called Lovers' Leap. Goram's Chair, the seat of a legendary giant, lies on the opposite hill shrouded by trees. Suburban Bristol lies in the middle distance, with Dundry Hill on the far horizon. Return to the tower and resume your direction.

Enter the woods at the far end of the down by the left-hand path. There is an orienteering mark (61) to your right. Go downhill. Cross over a junction in the paths and walk down the steps. After another cross path and more steps the recreation area appears below. The car park where you started lies on the left. Blaise Castle Folk Museum is to the right. There is an exit into Kings Weston Road on the left of the toilets for bus goers.

*Refreshments:* These are available at Blaise Castle and there is a provisions shop in Station Road. The Salutation pub in Henbury Road serves carvery style meals plus specials all day at reasonable prices and is only three or four minutes' drive away. The walk surfaces briefly in Sea Mills village, close to the shops.

## NOTES

**Blaise Castle:** The Folk Museum is housed in an 18th century mansion of sober design that was built for Quaker banker, John Scandrett Harford. It has an orangery of later date. Humphrey Repton landscaped the estate and it is one of three publicly owned parks in the country upon which he worked. He taught that grounds should be humanised, animated and cheerful. To put this into effect, he landscaped parks with irregularities and variety. Blaise Castle estate bears this out, with its many ups and downs.

Blaise Castle tower, the 18th century whimsy, was built as an ornamental feature. It was always an empty shell and was never meant to be inhabited. Restoration was carried out a few years ago.

Blaise Castle hamlet was the creation of architect John Nash, who designed it at the start of the 19th century for John Scandrett Harford, the wealthy banker already mentioned. It was built for the comfort of his personal servants during their retirement. It has been called 'Noddy Land' and 'a delightful essay in the picturesque' – two extreme comments; make of the hamlet what you will.

**Scipio Africanus** was brought to this country to act as a personal servant. The genuine grief of his master was expressed by Scipio being buried in a prominent part of the churchyard at Henbury St Mary. The 18th century trade in human cargo was mainly to North America but some slaves were purchased by sea port captains and traded to serve English masters as menials. It became something of a vogue to buy a black-skinned slave and dress him in the extravagant livery of the period.

**Bristol Portway** was built in 1926 to provide Bristol with a direct road link with Avonmouth Docks and, today, it also serves as an access link with the M5 motorway.

**Abonae** was the name given to the port built first in Roman times to provide a sea link for trading between Wales, Ireland and the south and west of England, long before Bristol came into existence. About 200 years ago it had a second life and flourished for a time, only to decline and fall into disuse.

# LONG ASHTON
# AND ASHTON PARK

*The deer park*

The urban surroundings of Ashton Park may not immediately suggest a scenic country walk in Bristol but this ramble, in fact, merits top rating. The undulations and splendid woodland combined with the views and charm of an old established estate add up to a very pleasant, but not too demanding, outing.

- **HOW TO GET THERE:** This walk starts at the Church Lodge Gate to Ashton Park. This is on the B3128 Bristol/Clevedon road opposite to the junction with the Long Ashton road. By bus – there are frequent buses passing by on weekdays on some of the services between Bristol and Weston-super-

Mare, and elsewhere. By car – from Bristol go through the Cumberland Basin and follow the A370 Weston-super-Mare road for $^3/_4$ mile then bear left to the B3128 Clevedon road. The park gates are on the right about $^1/_2$ mile further on (opposite to the road to Long Ashton village). Turn into the park gates and stop in the first lay-by on the left of the drive. Walk back down the drive through the ornate Victorian gates for the start of the walk.

- **LENGTH OF THE WALK:** $4^1/_2$ miles of comfortable terrain, taking about $2^1/_2$ hours. Maps: OS Landranger 172 Bristol & Bath or OS Explorer 154 Bristol West (GR 555713).

**THE WALK**

**1.** Cross into Long Ashton Road with All Saints' church set back on the left. Pass by the Angel Inn, which you will see on the left, and after a good 200 yards, turn right by the yew tree into Hobwell Lane (sign to golf course on the right wall of the lane). Continue forward until the road swings to the right and there is a farm and swing gate ahead. Go through the swing gate and follow a clear path to the left. At the field corner go left along the hedge to a further swing gate, and then into an enclosed path. It leads into Folleigh Drive. Go straight on and take the first right turn uphill (Folleigh Lane). Continue up until you see a left junction to Folleigh Close, and on your right a dwelling entrance to 'Pine Croft'.

**2.** Straight ahead is a narrow footpath signposted to the golf course. It goes uphill. Pass through a swing gate and almost immediately bear right upwards. At the next fork keep right and follow the path through the bracken hillside to the top and the golf course. There are good views of Dundry Hill.

Continue straight ahead over the fairway – there is a rather obscured waymark – passing a tree-shrouded pond on your left. Upon reaching the trees and tall evergreens on the far side turn left and walk the edge of the golf course (the trees now on your right). Keep on and ignore any paths on the right going into the scrub and woodland, also other sections of the golf course; again to your right. At the far end of the course (about $^3/_4$ mile) where

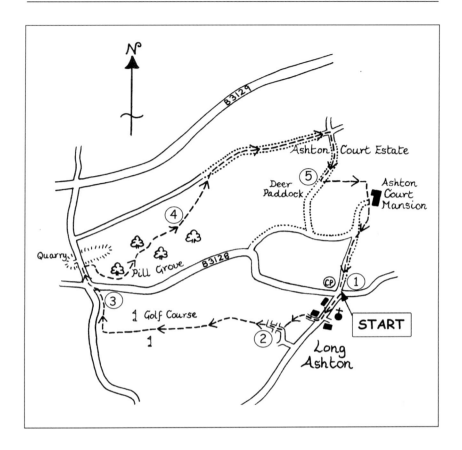

you meet a new boundary wall, turn right and follow this slightly downhill. The new wall is on your left, an open field is on the right.

At a path junction, take the narrow stepped centre track with a guide-rail uphill for a short way. It leads above a small disused quarry (now part of the golf course) and then on towards the right of a conical evergreen (the road and a wire fence are on your left). Take the short track into the road (Providence Lane).

**3.** Turn right uphill to the crossroads. Go over and walk straight on. Opposite to the quarry entrance turn right into a wood. This is Pill Grove and part of the Ashton Park estate.

Immediately take the right-hand broad track and walk slightly downhill through this very pleasant woodland. There are mixed beeches and pine – it is very reminiscent of the Chiltern woods. Continue forward until you meet a wide T-junction. There is a direction sign on your right. Turn left and walk for about 10 yards and just before the track goes uphill, there is a short narrow track off left with a yellow pole on the right. You will see open ground just ahead; continue forward. Leave the wood through a gap in the trees. Caution! There is a busy narrow path used by mountain bikers just at this point – take care. As you enter the meadow, to the left, a high bank and metal perimeter fence conceal and protect the quarry.

**4.** Proceed half right across this vast open pasture to the end of the wood, which you will see disappearing over the skyline. Here you will meet a track to take you in the same direction. The plantation on your right consists of young sycamores. At the T-junction turn right and walk the broad avenue through the park for $^1/_2$ mile. As the land falls away you will be rewarded with a vista of Leigh Woods to the left, the spire of Abbots Leigh church, then the broad truncated looking tower of Bristol University and the very slender Cabot tower. And, into the far distance – built-up Bristol. The broad avenue ends with a metalled drive. Turn right.

This very pleasant metalled drive undulates and takes you past some ancient dying and dead oaks on your left. In the same direction under the hill is a very fine view of Ashton Court mansion. The drive climbs over a hill where, at the top, starts the enclosed deer paddock. You can walk down the hill and look at the deer. Afterwards retrace your steps up the hill to the end of the deer enclosure.

**5.** Turn right and walk across the open grassland down to the Ashton Court mansion. Pass in front of the house towards the formal gardens and the fine tall redwoods. At the far end of the forecourt, go down the steps into the gardens. Pass by the redwoods to reach the rose garden beyond. If you look just over the drive from the redwoods, under a tree is the animal cemetery. When you are ready to leave this pleasant place, resume your direction by passing through the rose garden and beyond to reach the driveway. Continue for a few hundred yards to the lay-by where you left your car. Or, if you came by bus, continue along the drive to the entrance gates of the park.

*Refreshments:* The Angel Inn at Long Ashton, the café behind the mansion and in Ashton Park the café adjacent to the golf hut.

**NOTES**

**Long Ashton:** Before the complex structure of roads connecting Bristol's Cumberland Basin was built in the 1960s, Long Ashton was on the main road to Weston-super-Mare, then one of the busiest out of the city. Today it basks in a quieter atmosphere, but it is by no means a backwater as the village has grown with new housing and a fair-sized shopping centre. Until the decline of the Smyth family fortunes it was protected from urban sprawl and industrialisation, as it was the estate village of the family mansion. The original part of the village and the Angel Inn are passed on the walk. There are several old cottages, which form a cluster around the medieval church. Where Church Lane ends there is a good view back to the ornate castellated Victorian Gothic gatehouse that forms the entrance to Ashton Park. All Saints' church is of 14th century date and contains many monuments to the park owners. One angel-adorned tomb is that of Sir Richard Choke in his official regalia as Lord Chief Justice of England (died 1486).

The Smyth family originally came to Bristol from the Forest of Dean and traded as successful merchants, exporting goods to Ireland among other places. Matthew Smyth purchased the Long Ashton estate in 1545 from Sir Thomas Arundel for the bargain sum of £920. It included the manor house, the Chantry of Long Ashton, and very extensive lands. In all, it was a magnificent estate. They held Ashton Park and its very ornate mansion for some 400 years until the Bristol Corporation purchased it in 1959. Since then it has been a public park freely open to the general public. The mansion is a conference and function centre.

*Ashton Court Mansion*

The ancient park was probably first an enclosure for the animals of the chase and its antiquity may be judged from the several Tudor oaks now dying or dead in the open space above the mansion.

*WALK 14*

# COLD ASHTON AND ST CATHERINE'S VALLEY

*High Street, Marshfield*

The best of the high Cotswold landscape is featured in this
walk. Pasture predominates, and the lanes are narrow and
quiet. The clear air encourages colourful lichens, which,
coupled with the modest green mosses, thrive on the low
limestone walls. The route follows the Cotswold Way long
distance footpath for a time where it dives up and down along
the escarpment overlooking the broad vale leading to
Gloucester. After Cold Ashton the upper reaches of remote St
Catherine's valley give the feeling of a world apart, so silent
and tranquil is the setting.

- **HOW TO GET THERE:** By car – Marshfield is just off the A420 Bristol/Chippenham road approximately 14 miles east of Bristol. Parking can be found at the western end of the village. By bus – 2 hourly, from Bristol and Chippenham.
- **LENGTH OF THE WALK:** 7 miles; allow about 3 to 3¹/₂ hours. Maps: OS Landranger 172 Bristol & Bath or OS Explorer 155 Bristol & Bath (GR 771737).

### THE WALK

**1.** Starting from the western end of Marshfield's main street, take the lane opposite the old turnpike house and Green Lane cul-de-sac. Cross over the A420 main road where a lane leads to Westend Town Farm. At the first set of tall cottages the farm can be seen beyond a dip in the road. Pass two modern houses, the farm and Moonrakers Cottage. Where the lane ends in a Y junction, take the right-hand track. After a few yards where the way goes gently downhill, look for a waymarked double stile in the elevated walling on the right. It consists of an old stone stile and a modern wooden one. In the field beyond proceed downhill with the walling and track at first on your left.

As the wall and track fall away to the left continue forward down to the hollow where a waymarked stile leading to a footbridge will be seen. Note the middle of several poles carrying electricity cables; this shows your direction after crossing the little bridge. As you ascend the rising ground afterwards a stile will be seen beyond the middle electricity pole. This stile too is waymarked, but is in poor condition. After the stile go forward in the same direction to the far gate in the large meadow. Do not go through the gate but turn right before it into a green track barred by another gate. Beyond the gate the track leads uphill into a tarred lane.

**2.** Continue in the same direction along the lane for a mile to reach the A46 Bath/Nailsworth road. This is one of the highest parts of the walk at 730 ft. Turn right, cross the busy road and then left into a minor road leading to Dyrham village. Walk for about 100 yards down this road.

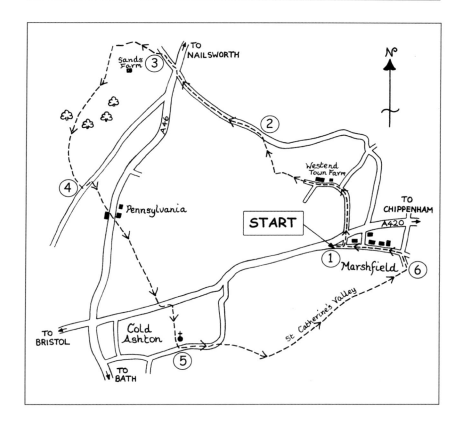

**3.** At two opposing gates take the left-hand one and stile and go downhill. The path has been diverted at this point. Follow the guidepost, and walk a clear path with the stonewalling and hedge on your left-hand. The view through the wedge-shaped opening in the lip of the plateau is very good. Pucklechurch will be seen in the middle distance.

The track continues downhill to the left of a cultivated field and briefly through a narrow wood. Sands Farm is below to your left. A waymark indicates a way through a large meadow overlooking the farm. At the meadow bottom, a waymark points to a gap in the wall, followed by a scramble down to a farm road; pass over this and through a new metal swing gate opposite. Follow the left-hand wall just past a walnut tree and through the next swing gate. Go diagonally across to and through the gate at the bottom left corner of the next field. Pass a pond on your left-hand side. Upon reaching the hedge on the far side of a cultivated field turn left. You are now on the waymarked Cotswold Way long distance footpath to take you to Cold Ashton.

The footpath passes under the plateau for a while in a southerly direction and then climbs up through Dyrham Wood. To reach the woods follow the defined footpath across a small combe and then through a narrow copse. (The OS map shows there was once a withy bed here.) Go slightly left uphill to reach a swing-gate in the far distant hedge corner. After the gate a pleasant gravel path leads up through the old coppiced trees of Dyrham Wood to open ground at a field corner. Keep the hedge on your left as you climb over the top of the slope to the signpost and roadway at the end of the field.

**4.** Turn left along the busy road for a short distance. At the signpost turn right and walk along the right-hand hedge of a large field. This will take you into a short enclosed way to the hamlet of Pennsylvania. Sadly the Swan is now only a B & B. There is a garage shop next to it.

Cross the A46 Bath/Nailsworth road to a gap opposite onto the Cotswold Way. Your path now goes diagonally up a large sloping field under crops to a stile in the left-hand corner. Continue half left to another stile and the A420 Bristol/Chippenham road at Cold Ashton. Cross the road and turn left along the far side. Opposite the White Hart, go through an iron swing gate and follow the grass verge between a drive and a stonewall. This crosses a drive into a short enclosed path. Go through the swing gate into the churchyard of Holy Trinity church.

**5.** Pass the church on your left and another swing gate into a way by the former school and into the road. Turn left. Here is where we leave the Cotswold Way. The view over St Catherine's valley is very good.

About 50 yards beyond the last house in the hamlet turn right through a heavy pair of gates. Follow the left-hand hedge downhill to a gate and continue down a steep green track. Beyond a further gate the track becomes enclosed and drops downwards below the field level. Continue to follow the right-hand hedge by the side of a pleasant green combe that will take you into St Catherine's valley and eventually to a ruined farmhouse on a bend in the valley. Walk the track past the crumbling building on your left-hand side and continue on through the long field to a gap. A second long field leads gently up the valley and ends with a hunting gate and stile alongside. There is now a brook on your right. Continue along the brook side into open ground. Pass the source of the brook going upwards in the same direction, now through scrub, into two clearings but keep with the course of the brook. Soon a barbed wire fence will bar the top of the valley. Go up the right-hand bank towards the trees and you will see a stone and wooden stile in the hedge in the field corner. Turn left into an enclosed track beyond (Green Lane).

When this track bends left, cross the stile ahead into a field and follow the clear path to a further stile in the right-hand corner.

**6.** Through the next field, walk half left to reach St Martin's Lane at the signposted stile and adjacent street lamp. Turn left to reach Marshfield's main street. Once more left will bring you back to the starting point of the walk.

*Refreshments:* The White Hart at Cold Ashton. There is a garage at Pennsylvania and shops and a pub in Marshfield.

### NOTES

**Marshfield** has a curious name for such a high exposed place but it has its origin in 'March' – a boundary. The village is now bypassed. Its grey limestone buildings are mostly of the 17th and 18th century. Some have distinctive canopied front doors. In the High Street are two old inns and also a noteworthy row of gabled 17th century almshouses founded by Elias Crispe. They consist of eight two-storey houses that now have a one-storey addition at the back to enable the occupants to enjoy modern amenities. There is a central chapel with clock tower. St Mary's church is at the eastern end of the village.

**Cold Ashton:** At 700 ft above sea level it is the highest village to be visited in this collection of walks and it lives up to its name. It lies just off the A420 Bath/Chippenham road. It is on record that Rector Thomas Key rebuilt Holy Trinity church in the 16th century, though he never divulged the secret of how he provided the means to do so. Inside the church is a brass to his memory. In the pleasant churchyard can be found tombs of the Whittington family, an offshoot of the line related to the famous Dick. It is worthwhile pausing during the walk to look at the hamlet. It contains a very handsome 17th century manor house built to the order of John Gunning, a wealthy Mayor of Bristol. It stands on the site of an even earlier one. The old school built in 1860 has been splendidly remodelled into a dwelling house.

# DUNKERTON
# AND PRISTON MILL

*Splott Farm Bridge*

Here is a ramble that lends itself to a closer look at the
wonderful rolling countryside that now lies over what was
once the Somerset coalfield. Two small coal slag hills, for
instance, can be passed unnoticed unless specially pointed out
and the scene now appears as if undisturbed apart from
agriculture; thus the farmer has proved that it is possible to
erase all traces of the district's industrial past. Yet another point
of interest is Priston Mill though it is only available for pre-
booked events. The walk goes through the mill yard, which lies
on the right of way.

- **HOW TO GET THERE:** By car – Dunkerton is 5 miles south of Bath on the A367 road to Radstock. Park in one of two lay-bys. There is one on each side of Dunkerton bridge in the Cam valley at a distance of a few hundred yards. By bus – weekdays, every 20 minutes. Any service from Bath bus station going via Radstock will stop at Dunkerton.
- **LENGTH OF THE WALK:** A hilly $5^1/_2$ miles, so allow $2^1/_2$ to $3^1/_2$ hours. Maps: OS Landranger 172 Bristol & Bath or OS Explorer 155 Bristol & Bath and Explorer 142 Shepton Mallet & Mendip Hills East (GR 716595).

### THE WALK

**1.** Go down the stone steps and through a dog-friendly stile on the south side of Dunkerton Bridge (on your right facing towards Radstock). Follow the footpath with the Cam brook on your right. The church of Dunkerton soon comes into view. It stands in a raised graveyard surrounded by several tall evergreens that dwarf the modest tower. Go between the graveyard and the brook to a swing gate.

Cross the lane and over a stone stile opposite. Continue forward with the brook on your right through several fields. In the fifth, pass between a wood-fenced pond and the brook, after which the village of Carlingcott can be seen on the skyline. In the middle distance lies the last visible indication of Dunkerton colliery in the form of a tree-clad hill naturalized from the coal-spoil heap. After passing under the electricity wires ignore the concrete bridge over the brook and walk forward to a stile in the spinney. A clear path then leads to the lane near the stone bridge. Continue in the same direction with Splott Farm on the left. After about 100 yards along the lane turn right (there is a grey post and electricity pole in the hedge opposite). A pleasant enclosed track then follows the brook. On your right is a close view of the old coal-spoil hill. Cross the brook by the concrete bridge and continue your direction on the other side of the water where a fenced (and perhaps muddy) way passes a vineyard. Go through a hunting gate at the end.

**2.** Bear right into the lane and proceed uphill out of the valley. The lane zigzags over the disused Somerset & Dorset railway line and then climbs steeply up to Tunley.

It is worthwhile looking back over the tranquil valley with Carlingcott and Lower Peasedown to be seen on the far slopes. Further along, Camerton church peeps from amongst its surrounding trees.

Tunley is a long narrow village on the ridge. We reach it at its western end. Cross the B3115. Turn right and pass the family butcher's shop, by the side of which an arched passageway leads to the back of the row of buildings. At the end turn right into a track that serves as a back lane to the houses. On your left is the long low coal-spoil heap of Tunley pit. It has a covering of green vegetation and scrub. There is a clear view of Priston below, which is the next objective on the walk. At the end of Tunley village, continue forward. Ignore the cross path. The bridleway narrows as it goes slightly downwards for nearly 200 yards.

**3.** At the cross track go left and follow it through a large unfenced field, at the far side of which go over a stile. Turn right and almost immediately left to walk downhill through open cultivated ground, with a ditch on your right, towards Priston. Pass under the electricity wires and proceed to the right of the house below. Here a stile gives access to a mossy metalled track. Follow it down beside the stream and then the house entrance drive to the lane below. Turn right over the rise in the lane (called Hillview) to take you into Priston. At the junction turn left and up into Priston Lane. Pass by the Ring O' Bells and the village hall. (A side lane here leads to the church.) Note the drinking fountain in the wall. Continue out of the village for some 300 or so yards where, at two right turns, there is a narrow lane to Priston Mill (signposted – $^1/_2$ mile).

**4.** Walk the lane to the mill. It lies in the next valley surrounded by large square cultivated fields. Walk through the mill yard to the far end and climb the stile into the pasture beyond. The walk now goes up out of the valley to Inglesbatch, which can be seen on the hillside ahead.

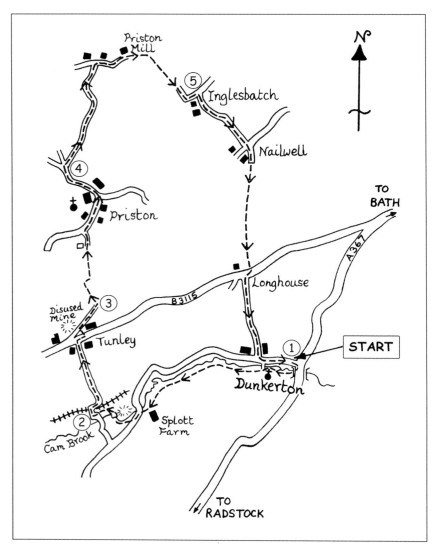

Walk through the pasture to the electricity pole. Follow the overhead cable to the stream; there is a faint path. Continue along the left bank to the pasture corner; there is a footbridge. Cross over into the field beyond. Follow the wire fencing and hedge on your right for a few yards, no more than 20, then cross the stile. It is partly hidden in the hedge next to a young hazel tree. Climb uphill through a large meadow. The electricity supply cable is again in view and provides an excellent direction pointer. The footpath actually follows the cable up the field. At the top of the meadow a good track called Mill Lane leads to the hamlet of Inglesbatch.

**5.** At the stainless-steel telephone box turn right. Inglesbatch is small and you will soon leave the buildings behind. Continue up the narrow bendy lane to Nailwell ($1/2$ mile).

Nailwell is another place that scarcely merits the title of hamlet. The walk passes its eastern end. At the lane junction, go straight over into a cul-de-sac by Nailwell House. Beyond the second house the track becomes the width of a footpath. Where the end is blocked follow the path through a new metal hunting gate on your right up into the open field. Resume your direction up the side of Duncorn Hill. The hedge-line is now on your left. Continue on through a field gate and meadow. To your right over the open cultivation the view is superb. In the far distance the hummocky hills near to Farmborough Common go by the name of The Oozles. Nearer to hand Priston nestles into a fold in the landscape. Here at something over 560 ft above sea level it feels as though this should be the highest point of the walk, though in reality it is no more lofty than Tunley passed earlier.

In about $1/2$ mile the path is gated, becoming a track once more for a very short distance as it nears the road at Longhouse (B3115). Turn right, cross over the road, and immediately take the left of two lanes to go steeply downhill. Dunkerton church and village will be seen straight ahead in the valley below. It is a pretty setting. The lane passes the village hall and goes by the name of The Hollow, which is apt. There was once a high viaduct carrying the railway but this has gone and the only reminder to be seen is Viaduct Cottage. Turn left at the junction near to the bridge and walk the lane alongside the brook to Dunkerton Bridge, where you began the walk.

*Refreshments:* The Ring O' Bells pub in Priston.

*Priston Mill*

## NOTES

**Priston Mill** has the appearance of being very much a permanent feature, which indeed, it is as it was first mentioned in the *Domesday Book*. There cannot be many to boast such a record. The present mill has an iron overshot pitch back wheel of between 130 and 150 years of age. It has a diameter of 27 ft and 10 inches, which, in its very dark setting under the building, appears twice as large. All around was once a system of water-fed meadows controlled by sluices that kept the fields moist in dry weather. The mill-house nearby goes back to the 18th century. Casual visitors are no longer welcome. The mill caters for corporate events and marriages.

**Priston** sits very comfortably into a wooded setting. It has a prosperous air and a good infilling of modern houses. The church has several ancient features. What receives most remarks is the lively weathercock on the tower. It has been called 'fat-bottomed' and 'over large' but with such proportions it certainly holds a special sentimental attachment for the village. In the Middle Ages the weathercock was said to be on watch at all times to dispel sin and the noisy crowing of the real bird at dawn kept evil away.

**The Somerset Coalfield:** The places where coal measures were laid down 200 million years ago are sometimes flat and monotonous, as with the area immediately to the north-east of Bristol. By contrast, the old Somerset coalfield lies under a verdant undulating landscape, which is probably why the seams tended to be tilted and full of faults. It never attracted heavy industry, as yields from the thin seams were not of the highest quality. Some of the produce was made into coke and the rest went elsewhere. The coalfield working finally ceased about 30 years ago. Around 1900 the workforce was over 6,000, which shows the flexibility of the people in coming to terms with change and a different means of earning a living.

**Dunkerton** is an attractive village. Its last colliery was the largest in the district soon after it had opened in 1905. Bad working conditions caused riots in 1908/9 and continual financial problems caused its working life to be short. It closed in 1925.

# CHEW VALLEY LAKE AND CAMELEY

❧❦❧

*Prospect stile*

This elevated walk among the outlying hills of the northern Mendips provides some marvellous views. One of the satisfying things about the Chew Lake is that it can be looked down upon from several places, and on a clear day the dramatic setting of the sparkling waters in the Chew valley is most enjoyable. The walk winds among the small hills which curl around the south-east side of the lake, and then visits the almost deserted village of Cameley. Hinton Blewett is also in a particularly beautiful part of the Cam valley. If you do this walk in autumn you will not be disappointed; the colours around the Chew Valley, in particular, are magnificent.

- **HOW TO GET THERE:** By car – North Widcombe is a thin scattering of houses just off the A368 Bath/Weston-super-Mare road, halfway between Bishop Sutton and West Harptree; it is on your left just before Herriott's Bridge, which crosses the south tip of Chew Valley Lake. Park carefully by the small green or at the side of the road. By bus – there is Chew Valley Explorer stop at the North Widcombe turning (Bristol to Cheddar service 672, 673 or 674) and four buses daily on the Bristol/Burrington service. Walk forward from the stop and take the first left. The small green is a few yards forward on your left.
- **LENGTH OF THE WALK:** 6$^1/_2$ miles, which will take about 4 hours. Maps: OS Landranger 182 or OS Explorers 141 Cheddar Gorge & Mendip Hills West and 142 Shepton Mallet & Mendip Hills East (GR 575584).

## THE WALK

**1.** Start at the North Widcombe turn-off on the A368. With your back to the road and houses, cross the small green and go up the tarmac track which ascends Burledge Hill. After Hart's Farm Cottage, this soon becomes stony with considerable traces of the fossils common to limestone areas. On reaching the open green triangle of ground at the top, turn left but keep up close to the hedge, now on your right, as there is no obvious track at first. However, the way soon becomes an enclosed wide, but slightly overgrown path, which after a good $^1/_4$ mile ends with a waymarked stile onto Burledge Common, where there is a fine panorama of the Chew Valley lake in its bowl-like setting. Denny Island is to the right. The long straggling village immediately below the hill is Bishop Sutton.

Follow the right-hand hedge and fence to the Ordnance Survey triangulation point marking the top of the common. From here, walk down the field half left to a new wooden gate in the boundary hedge (near to the wood in the bottom corner). After the gate there is a distinct path with new steps that contours the hill. At the foot of the steps and after a gate, follow the clear footpath that leads to a stile. There are more steps downwards passing under overhead wires. At the bottom

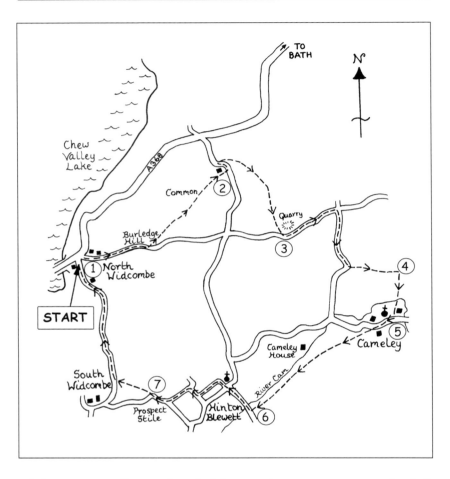

of the steps go forward and right passing a waypost on the left towards a modern cottage. Pass it on the left over a stile.

**2.** Turn left for a short distance down the hill, and then over a stile on your right. There is a new field gate in front of you; ignore this, instead turn right, with a wire fence on the left, and go through the new metal gate ahead into a large field.

Walk the faint footpath forward over the rise and pass under the overhead wires, in the direction of the middle wood of three ahead. There is a footbridge over a stream. Cross the water. Take the rightmost of two paths immediately in front. This takes you up and to the right as you wend your way up the shallow valley. Pass through a gate half way up and follow a curved track up to the top left corner, passing an active landfill on the right. At the top corner of the field go through a gate and turn left onto the road. There is a very fine view back from where you have come.

**3.** Pass the quarry on the left. After a third of a mile, turn right at the road junction into a bridleway called Nanny Hum's Lane. This pleasant track goes southwards for $^3/_4$ mile when it suddenly bends to the right and goes downhill. Do not continue but go through the gate ahead and turn left into a rough overgrown field.

Follow the top of the hill in an easterly direction. There is a lovely view of the Cam valley with Cameley church and lake below. After nearly $^1/_2$ mile the rough pasture ends in a gate and 'X' stile. Don't cross into the next field here, instead turn right following the hedge and wire fence on your left down through scrub and undergrowth for a short while. Go through two waymarked gates (currently in poor condition) and resume your original direction for a short way along the top of a field.

**4.** After passing an oak (the top one of three in a line) and before reaching the wood, turn right through the large field and go down towards the bottom of the valley. Cameley church is below on your right.

At the bottom of the large field do not go through the gate but head in the direction of the small grey stone ruined wall. Pass this by on your left-hand side where a rough green track leads down to the brook. It is the River Cam, which will be met again. Cross by the footbridge. St James's church is now fairly near on your right. Walk through the field and head to the left of the farm (but right of the barn), where you will find a new metal swing gate in the fence. Pass through a yard into the road. Turn right into the lane.

**5.** Cameley church is now only a few yards along the metalled lane. After leaving it behind continue along the lane for a good $^1/_4$ mile. After passing a small bridge on a slight bend (barn on left) pass through a gate on the left. Ascend diagonally right through the field to a stile on the hill plainly in view. After the stile continue in the same direction up the hill towards the wood. Pass under the power lines and continue up to the top, passing the wood on your right-hand side. The left hedge briefly drops away; when it returns the stile on the left comes into view.

Hinton Blewett village, which is the next objective, soon comes into view. Climb the gate in the far corner of the field. On your right in a dip is the Cam brook again. Through the trees lies Cameley House.

The well-used way now follows the Cam brook towards Hinton Blewett. There are pastures with three stiles/swing gates, the last of which is an old stone one. This or the gate gives access to the lane.

**6.** Turn right uphill to the village. The Ring O' Bells, St Margaret's church and the houses stand by an attractive green. Pass the church with its small neat tower on your right. Follow the metalled lane to a T-junction. Turn right leaving the village behind and continue along the lane which bends to the left before ending in another T-junction. Turn right once more and very soon on the next bend a very broad stile is reached. There is a wonderful view of Chew Lake and beyond, which has caused this place to be well named 'Prospect Stile'.

**7.** Pass over the stile. From here the path is not well defined. Your general direction is downward to the road plainly in view below and to the right of the small red house. There is first a very steep section downhill over rough ground, which is best tackled by walking to the waymarked telephone pole which will point you to the stile in the hedgerow beneath you; head for this. After the stile a further one will be seen in the next field. On the way pass near to the spring surrounded by trees and bushes. From the second stile the way to the road is plain to see.

Turn right into the road and pass Heyden's Farm left. The road has wide grass verges and an occasional large unenclosed space; these are the last remnants of the one-time common. From here it is about 1 mile back to North Widcombe and the starting place of the walk.

*Refreshments:* The Ring O' Bells in Hinton Blewett and the Butchers Arms at Bishops Sutton. There are also shops at Bishop Sutton and the Manor Farm Shop on the A368, opposite the turning to North Widcombe.

NOTES

**North Widcombe** is one of the small hamlets so common in this part of Avon where, in the 19th century, country people migrated into the larger villages and towns looking for a better living.

**Cameley** is another, once large enough to support a church. The inhabitants drifted to Temple Cloud a mile or so to the east where there was a main road for easier travel and communication and where work could be found in the coal and iron mines, the brickworks and the quarry. The red sandstone church of St James, Cameley, has earned the title of a Rip Van Winkle church, one that went to sleep for 150 years. In doing so it avoided the zealous Victorian improvers and has a gallery which last had a facelift in 1819. There are many Jacobean features including a rare Royal Coat of Arms of Charles I. The pulpit has a sounding board and there are several old box pews. It has a font of the 11th century and the north wall shows traces of a painting of great antiquity. The redundant church cared for by the Churches Conservation Fund is often open to visitors.

Cameley House (late Georgian) nearby has attractive two-storey Gothic Revival windows.

**Hinton Blewett** has all the attributes of a charming hamlet complete with public house, church and village green. The church is built of Doulting stone and has an interesting interior with many treasures, from a Norman font to 15th century benches.

**Bishop Sutton** lies on the eastern side of Chew Valley. From Burledge Common it looks like a commuter village with much modern infilling but there is also a close-knit nucleus. In the 18th century there were two main occupations: farming and coalmining. In 1750 there were four pits when most of the output was used for re-smelting in the Mendip lead mines. The last pit closed in 1929 due to flooding.

**Burledge Hill** has an Iron Age fort and a possible Roman encampment though little of the earthworks is visible through the scrub and trees.

**Chew Valley Lake** looks natural though it is an artificial reservoir opened by Queen Elizabeth in 1956 to serve Bristol's increasing demand for water. It is scientifically stocked with brown and rainbow trout that attract anglers from all over the world. Other leisure time pursuits are catered for in the small boat sailing and bird watching. Many species of bird gratefully seize upon what has become an oasis for them and a feast for the people who watch. Migratory birds include a small flock of Bewick swans that winter in this country.

# WRINGTON
# AND THE YEO VALLEY

*Yeo weir*

An opportunity to ramble through well preserved woodland is always enjoyable. Here is a walk that climbs through the hilly parts to the north of the main Mendip fringe. It overlooks the pretty Yeo Valley and there are good views of the green and tawny brown Mendips. The route skirts Congresbury and follows the Yeo river for a time. The reach to the west of Wrington is particularly pleasant.

- **HOW TO GET THERE:** By car – Wrington lies 1 mile west of the A38 Bristol/Bridgwater road at Redhill, about 12 miles south-west of Bristol. There is parking in Broad Street. By

bus – hourly weekdays on the Bristol/Weston-super-Mare
service via Bristol airport.
- **LENGTH OF THE WALK:** $5^1/_4$ miles, so allow $2^1/_2$ to 3 hours.
Maps: OS Landranger 172 Bristol & Bath or OS Explorer 154
Bristol West & Portishead (GR 469629)

THE WALK

**1.** With your back to the parish church at Wrington, proceed
along Broad Street, passing the Golden Lion Inn near to the bus
stop on your left. Turn left into High Street and climb the hill.
Pass by the Plough Inn and the village pump. After a bend in the
road turn right into a metalled footway between 'Yeomans' and
'Southcombe'. It climbs between tall walls and comes out into a
lane. Turn left for a short distance. Pass by 'Lilac Cottage' and,
opposite to the United Reformed church, turn right into a
signposted public footpath called Bullhouse Lane. It goes uphill
and, after passing 'Long Orchard', becomes a tree-lined track.
There is a lovely view over the Yeo valley.

**2.** The track ends in a T-junction. Turn left into the minor road
and walk past Oatlands, consisting of a small cluster of buildings
on the left – there are hardly sufficient for it to be called a
hamlet. At this point the road enters the eastern side of
Corporation Woods, and in $^1/_4$ mile the edge of the wood can be
seen.

**3.** Turn left at the sign to Woolmers Kennels. (There is an
interesting old boundary stone here marked 'Manor of
Congresbury'.) The drive bears left around the back of
Woodside Cottage and then right to penetrate Woolmers Wood.
It is a good $^3/_4$ mile through this very pleasant mature woodland
before a couple of clearings are reached. Go straight on past
Woolmers Farm with its pleasant gardens and the kennels.
The way now changes into a very pleasant broad path. It is
easy to follow and has a good firm surface. Presently, after a cross
track, the way goes gently downhill. Continue forward passing a
waymark post; at times the path narrows and runs between
quite step banks. Ignore any paths coming into the main one

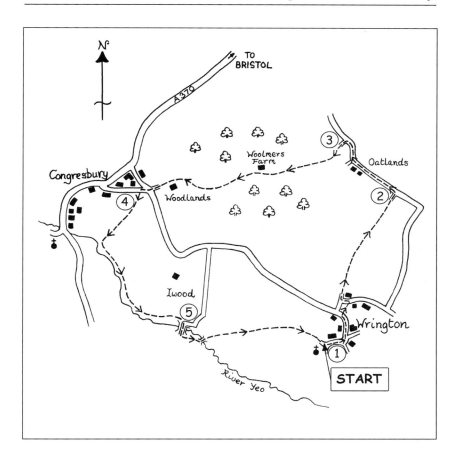

being followed. After 1 mile the end of the wood is reached and the way turns into a metalled driveway, passing Woodlands Lodge (right) shortly to reach the road at a T-junction. The large house adjacent is called 'Woodlands'. There are extremely pleasant views of Congresbury valley with the village in the middle distance and Wavering Down and Crook Peak far away on the horizon. They are easily distinguishable by their names, and Crook Peak is sometimes called the Matterhorn of the South-west. Cross the road, turn left, and immediately after Wrington Lane go over a field stile. Here is another very fine glimpse of Congresbury church in the middle of the village lying to the right.

**4.** Walk across the field to the next stile, keeping to the left of some rough high ground, in the fence just ahead. Go diagonally right to a third stile, also visible next to the ash tree. Now continue forward and pass the double poles carrying the electricity supply cables to a gap in the hedge beyond. There is now a clear path leading to the Congresbury Yeo riverside (hedge on right). Turn left onto the riverbank, passing the weir and keeping the river on the right side. Do not confuse the River Yeo with a small narrow stream that you will encounter first.

The next part of the walk is along this very pleasant and quiet valley. There is a well-worn path at first, which goes away from Congresbury along the water's edge. On the left is a good view of the woods through which you have walked and to the right lies the long ridge of the Mendips. Continue along the riverbank and ignore any crossings for a good mile. Every bend of the river presents a new picture and it is very pleasant to linger. Pass by the Somerset River Authority gauging station to reach the lane at Iwood. This is a very small hamlet, consisting of a couple of farms and a manor.

**5.** Turn right over the double-arched river bridge to reach the southern side of the water. Here there is a signpost pointing to Wrington. Climb the stile and walk the riverbank with the water on your left. After several hundred yards the large meadow ends in a fence and a gate. Ignore both and turn left to the riverbank where a narrow footbridge spans the river Yeo. Cross over and walk away from the water.

Cross the meadow under the electricity wires where there is a stile in the right-hand corner. Now follow the left-hand hedge under more wires. Passing by a gate go slightly left where the path is faintly visible towards the next gate and stile. The tall, beautiful church tower of All Saints, Wrington, is now in full view ahead. Resume your direction along the hedge, now on your right. Pass under the electricity wires near to the tall pylon. Go through a gate beyond and then climb over a stile almost immediately on your right. Resume direction once more. Keep up close to the hedge on the left until your come to a stile in the corner. Now cross the open field and pass by the electricity

*The Plough Inn, Wrington*

poles, after which there will be a wet ditch with a wall and hedge on your right; note the play area top left. In the bottom field corner pass through an old iron swing gate into an enclosed pathway, which will bring you out into Ladywell cul-de-sac in Wrington village. Turn left to reach the parish church, The Triangle and Broad Street where the walk commenced.

*Refreshments:* The Plough Inn and the Walled Garden coffee shop, both at Wrington.

### NOTES
**Wrington** lies beneath Broadfield Down on the northern side of the low-lying Yeo Valley. Broad Street lives up to its name and is lined with pleasant 18th century buildings. It is worthwhile looking around this quiet orderly old market town. Time was when it was not so peaceful for in the early years of the 19th century it gained a reputation for lawlessness. The Mendip

119

miners who lived locally were blamed for the general disorderly behaviour.

It was into their homes and those of the agricultural labourers that Hannah More and her four sisters intruded in an effort to bring a little reading and religion into their narrow lives. These remarkable ladies sought to teach the grown-ups as well as the children. For the womenfolk Friendly Societies were started. The More sisters also endeavoured to improve the living conditions of the workers but their motives were distrusted. The clergy and gentry disapproved and resented what was regarded as an unnecessary interference. Hannah More lived between 1745 and 1833. In addition to her work as a social reformer she was highly esteemed for her literary talents, these included plays, and moral and religious tracts. She is buried with her four sisters in Wrington churchyard.

Another local celebrity was **John Locke**, the 17th century materialistic philosopher. It is said that on behalf of the Royal Society he once tried to take a barometer down a Mendip lead mine to see what happened to air pressure below ground. His efforts were to no avail though as the suspicious miners refused to let him go down. In many ways he was ahead of his time, especially in pressing for educational opportunities for children. His essay on *Human Understanding* is respectfully mentioned these days rather than read. His birthplace was a cottage near to the north gate of Wrington's churchyard.

**Wrington's old church** has a splendid two-stage west tower of over 113 ft in height. When the Houses of Parliament were rebuilt in 1835 after their destruction by fire, it is recorded that the architect, Sir Charles Barry, used the proportions of Wrington's tower as the basis for his design of the Victoria Tower. He also designed, in 1832, the reredos in the church. It is built of Caen stone.

Between Redhill and Wrington lies the **Barley Wood Estate**, until the 1970s the home of Henry Wills, a director of Imperial Tobacco. The Kitchen Gardens were split from the rest of the estate and purchased by the present owners in 1993.

The garden was constructed in 1901; the design was that of earlier Victorian times when these gardens were at their zenith. The garden was purchased in a considerable state of decay and neglect. Work commenced in clearing the land and May 1998 saw the start of the reconstruction of the Barley Wood **Walled Garden**. Brick and gravel paths were relaid and edging stones put back. Since then the fruit stores and workshops have been rebuilt, new trees planted, the derelict greenhouses totally re-glazed and renovated and window-winding gear made to work once more.

In the autumn of 1999, the Head Gardener and his assistant began the task of researching and planning the garden as far as possible as it would have been at the start of the 20th century.

# STANTON DREW STONE CIRCLE AND NORTON MALREWARD

◈

*The thatched toll house*

The fertile Chew Valley offers many opportunities for good outings. Here is one that follows the pleasant river meadows and then skirts the lower slopes of Dundry Hill. It is an area that has experienced man's taming influence over many hundreds of years since the Bronze Age when he started to scratch the soil and farm for his living. During the earlier part of this century it was renowned for its butter and cheese when milk and stock rearing predominated. Today's diversification has brought a nursery and market gardening, while on the slopes of Dundry there is an area of large-scale cereal production. Here the field boundary removal gives the landscape a completely new aspect, but not on so large a scale as to change its character.

- **HOW TO GET THERE:** By car – Pensford is south of Bristol on the A37 Shepton Mallet road. There is parking in Church Street. By bus – an hourly service, Bristol, Wells, Street, Yeovil, passes through Pensford. On alighting from the bus walk to the Chew Bridge and turn into Church Street.
- **LENGTH OF THE WALK:** 5 miles, which should take about 2 to 3 hours. Maps: OS Landranger 172 Bristol & Bath or OS Explorer 155 Bristol & Bath (GR 618638).

**THE WALK**

**1.** In Church Street go through the opening on the right of the Rising Sun inn. Turn left into the car park. At the far end on the right, close to the River Chew, you will find a stone stile; from here proceed over the Chew by the old stone mill bridge. Follow the riverbank under the very impressive and high 16-arch railway viaduct (built 1873).

Go forward to a waymarked swing gate, cross and ascend a slight rise to pick up a clear grassy track. A further swing gate leads to a small field and another swing gate conducts you nearer to the river. Continue towards the old mill, now a private dwelling house. Close to the water there are some very fine alders.

Go through the gate on the left of the house into the lane. Go forward immediately over the stile opposite. Follow the riverbank on your right. The waymarked path will take you through the meadows and over several stiles, gradually moving away from the river. When the lane is reached turn right. (Here the waymarks end.) Follow this quiet and narrow lane round a gentle left bend for a short way.

**2.** At two opposing gates turn right into a market garden. The footpath is through the cultivations. Ahead will be seen the church tower of Stanton Drew towards which you should go. Walk through several merged cultivated fields. Ahead is a tall hedge. Turn left at the hedge, walk up with the hedge on the

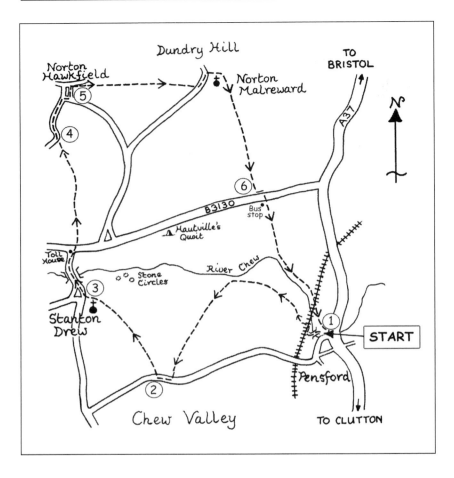

right to climb the slightly concealed waymarked stile in the hedge into the next field. Turn right and head for the broad track; join it at the sewage farm entrance. Turn left and it will take you again towards the church via a farmyard into the road. On your right there is an excellent view of the famed Stanton Drew stone circle. The entrance to the circle is in the hamlet.

**3.** To continue the walk turn right and follow the road out of the buildings past Stanton Court. Cross the River Chew by the ancient stone bridge (14th century) and walk towards the thatched tollhouse that stands in the middle of the road junction. Cross the busy B3130 Pensford/Chew Magna Road to the stile into a field just to the left of the garage. The next part of the walk climbs the lower slopes of Dundry Hill and goes through the hamlets of Norton Hawkfield and Norton Malreward.

Walk to the crest of the rising ground over two stiles – the first is plain to see, the second is tucked in the top left corner of the field. The view over the Chew Valley is magnificent with Pensford and its viaduct to the east and, to the south, the stone circle framed in deciduous trees. Continue forward and another good aspect comes into full prominence with Dundry Hill and Maes Knoll Iron Age hill fort forming a backcloth.

In the hollow beneath lies Norton Hawkfield with the squat church tower of Norton Malreward to the east. The setting is most attractive. Go slightly right to a stile in the hedge. The next stile is also slightly right but, since the field is cultivated, it may be easier to walk two sides of the planted area by following the left-hand hedges. After the stile walk along the left-hand hedge. When it ceases continue forward and slightly right to the last stile before the sunken roadway.

**4.** Turn right along the lane into the pretty hamlet of Norton Hawkfield. It has lost its church but the site was to the right of the lane. Beyond the brook turn right at the road junction (signposted Whitchurch/Bristol). The walk now turns east towards Norton Malreward and goes through the outer park of Norton Malreward Court.

**5.** At the end of the hamlet of Norton Hawkfield turn right into the entrance to Park Farm (bungalow called 'Highcroft' on right). Before reaching the farmhouse bear left along a broad waymarked track into the park. Walk forwards; there is a light wire fence to your left and open countryside to your right. At the end of the fence and at the waymark turn left and continue again with the fence on your left. Pass a group of horse chestnut trees on the right. There is now an iron fence on the left and a single tall evergreen redwood tree in the middle of the field to the left. In front of the tree will be seen an iron kissing gate. Go through the gate – it gives access to a track down to the brook and spinney. Cross the bridge in the dip to reach the road. Turn left. Pass Chalk Farm (now a housing estate), into Norton Malreward and past the payphone on the left.

Where the road bears left by the red post box in the stonewalling turn right towards the church. (Notice the damson tree and very large yew.) Before the entrance to the churchyard bear left past Manor Farm. (This very elegant, classical-style mansion has been very well restored within the last few years.) After the house go straight towards the newly converted barn dwelling. Turn right in front of the barn (blue waymark on wall); the way is obvious. Next comes an open cultivated area with a good well-drained track; go straight ahead (ignore any waymarked tracks to your left or right) through this big-big field. Follow this track forward for a good $1/2$ mile to reach the edge of the scarp with Chew Valley beyond. There is a gap in the hedgerow. Take the stony track that goes steeply downhill.

**6.** Upon reaching the B3130 Pensford/Chew Magna Road turn left (there is a footpath diversion in place here). Almost immediately turn right by the bus stop post. Go through the swing gate on the right, into the sheep pasture. Follow the left-hand fence and it will take you downwards and over a double stile into the riverside pastures. Here turn left and follow the bank-side towards Pensford. The path joins a track that climbs slightly uphill through pleasant newly developing woodland (Forest of Avon) before passing under the high viaduct. It leads to Church Street where the walk commenced.

*Refreshments:* Stanton Drew hamlet has the Druid's Arms inn. There are also shops and two pubs in Pensfold, the Rising Sun and the George & Dragon which is open all day.

## NOTES

The **River Chew**, which rises in the Mendips, has long been used for diverse water-powered small industries. Pensford village provides a good example where several mills were fed by intricate water channels crossed by quaint bridges. Along with

*The route passes under this viaduct near Pensford*

its old buildings and ancient church (now a cultural centre) it shows a period of prosperity back to the 16th century when the West of England wool trade predominated and when the dyeing and fulling of cloth was done in the village. Coal mining took over in the last century but this too has ceased. The small mines have closed and the spoil heaps have greened over to blend in unobtrusively with the surroundings.

**Stanton Drew:** This hamlet's main claim to fame is the circle of standing stones connected with the ancient Celtic priesthood, but nothing is known of the Bronze Age people who set them in position in the valley. There are said to have been three circles with two avenues of stones, though all that remains of them now presents an irregular pattern. As a focal point of curiosity they well serve the valley, not to mention their regular use as cattle rubbing posts. Legend has it that the Devil, in the guise of a fiddler, played for a wedding feast and caused the dancers to continue long after they should have done. When the Sabbath dawned the Devil had departed but he left the merrymakers petrified into the stones we see today.

On a tiny three-cornered patch of grass at the junction to the hamlet stands a unique hexagonal dwelling house, complete with thatched roof. It claims to date back to the 15th century. Three hundred years later it served as a tollhouse, a reminder of the days of the Turnpike Trusts, which extracted money from road users with vehicles and animals. The revenue collected was used for maintenance and for new thoroughfares.

Norton Malreward is overlooked by Dundry Hill, crowned on its eastern top by the Iron Age camp called Maes Knoll. Running up to it lie the vestigial remains of the Wansdyke which formed a boundary marker and stretched from the Bristol Channel as far east as the Savernake Forest.

Norton Hawkfield has a tale of Sir John Hautville, a knight whose great strength was renowned. Legend has it that he grabbed a huge stone from Maes Knoll and hurled it towards Stanton Drew. It landed in a field and is known to this day as Hautville's Quoit, though in reality the stone forms part of the older complex of the stone circle.